To Fran
Juvene

ROOTS LOST
ROOTS FOUND

With my Compliments
and in Friendship

Otto
Waterford, Rossmoor
Aug. 15, 2017

ROOTS LOST ROOTS FOUND

Otto Schnepp

Walnut Creek, California

Otto Schnepp
3838 Terra Granada Drive
Walnut Creek, CA, 94595

Cover design and interior layout by Ruth Schwartz,
aka My Book Midwife, mybookmidwife, com
based on a template © BookDesignTemplates.com

Cover illustration by Tali Burry-Schnepp

ROOTS LOST – ROOTS FOUND/ Otto Schnepp — 1st ed.
ISBN 978-1-5450688-8-5

Dedication

For my grandmother, Amalia Roth

Acknowledgements

I have written these memoirs to inform family and friends of my recollections of life in different countries where I have lived. It is significant to me how I happened to live there and how I happened to get to these particular countries.

I particularly wish to memorialize the role my grandmother played in my life. Unfortunately, we did not succeed to get her out of Vienna and to reunite with us in China. I realized only in later life that she played a key role as a role model of stability in my life.

I also wish to stress that she provided the money that allowed us all to reach our place of refuge in Shanghai and to escape the so-called Holocaust. In a sense, she provided the means for our survival. I wish to dedicate this book to her.

I also wish to acknowledge the considerable help I received from a number of sources that enabled me to write this memoir. My former wife, Eileen, encouraged me to join the Rossmoor Writing Club where I acquired a great deal of my writing skills with the support of Mary Webb, the Club's facilitator and principal guide. I further wish to acknowledge the encouragement I received from my good friend and long time collaborator, Marilyn Davin as well as my friend Barbara Becker.

Table of Contents

Introduction 1

My Early Years 5

Musical Experiences 19

Under Nazi Rule 29

Voyage to Shanghai and Our Beginnings There 35

Shanghai After Pearl Harbor.........................49

Triumph 63

Ghoya and the Pass 71

Liberation 81

Leaving Shanghai...95

From Shanghai to San Francisco...................107

Berkeley...119

From Berkeley to Israel 125

Adventures in the Israeli Army Reserves 139

Tragedy Strikes 147

Rise and Fall..157

Otto The Diplomat Part 1.............................173

Otto The Diplomat Part 2.............................191

Nepal Trek 199

Arieh and the Nobel Prize 235

The Women in My Life 253

Introduction

This is a memoir describing my life from my early years in Vienna, the city where I was born. At age 13, my life was forcefully disrupted by the Anschluss or Annexation of Austria by Nazi Germany in March 1938. As Jews, our family had to flee and was separated and displaced. My sister, Herta, was the first member of the family to leave Vienna; she emigrated to Kenya in East Africa where we had an uncle who found her a job. This gave her permanent residency in this British colony. My parents and I left Vienna in November 1938 and January 1939 for Shanghai's International Settlement, which at the time had no limitations on immigration and, as a result, served as a refuge for about 20,000 Jewish refugees from Germany, Austria and Poland.

Otto Schnepp

I lived in Shanghai with my parents throughout WWII and under Japanese military occupation after Pearl Harbor. I graduated from a United States Episcopalian missionary-founded college, St. John's University, in chemistry in 1947.

After the end of WWII in 1948, I left Shanghai for Berkeley where I completed my studies at the University of California with a Ph.D. in chemistry in 1951. In 1952 I went to live in Haifa, Israel, where I joined the faculty of the Israel Institute of Technology, also known as Technion. At Technion I rose through the ranks to a full professorship.

In 1965 I left Israel and moved to Los Angeles where I joined the faculty of the University of Southern California (USC) Chemistry Department in Los Angeles. I retired from the USC Chemistry Department in 1992 but returned in 1994 to take up the position of Director of the East Asian Studies Center and I retired from this position in December 2000. The East Asian Studies Center is not a department, but it is a collection of faculty specializing in Chinese, Japanese and Korean language and culture. It was my responsibility and challenge to obtain funding in support of the faculty members' and graduate students' scholarly activities. The funding came from the United States government Department of Education and private sources.

In 2007 I moved with my wife, Eileen, to the retirement community of Rossmoor in Walnut Creek, CA. Eileen died of peritoneal malignancy in December 2010. I have continued to live in Rossmoor and participate in various activities in this community.

Chapter 1

My Early Years

In the aftermath of World War I, Vienna was the impoverished capital of a much-diminished country that had once been the powerful Austro-Hungarian Empire. The Empire was dismembered after the defeat of the allied armies of Austria, Germany and Turkey by the Western European allies led by Great Britain, France and the United States. I was born in this city in July of 1925. We lived in a rented apartment in one of the poorer districts whose population was primarily working class. It also was known as one of the two heavily Jewish districts located on an island created by the large river, the Danube, and a much narrower artificial canal dug some centuries before to facilitate transportation by barge. In the fall, I saw barges laden with fruit — apples, plums, cherries, peaches, apricots and grapes. I remember the cargo as color-ful and spread out on the decks covering large areas contained only by partitions. In some places, the barges were accessible and people bought the fruit, retail, directly from these boats.

The Jews of Vienna hailed from the far reaches of the Empire. My father was born in Vienna, but his father was born in Lemberg, now called L'viv, a rela-tively large city in what is now the Ukraine, but at the time was a Polish city, called L'vov, located in Galicia, a province of the Empire before WWI. My mother was born in Budapest, Hungary and her family moved to Vienna in 1900 when she was six. Her father was a mechanical engineer, a self-made man, who was employed by a company headquar-tered in Budapest, the capital of Hungary. He was transferred to the Vienna branch, all within the Em-pire; it was like moving to another state here in the United States except that they spoke a different and unrelated language. However, my grandparents spoke faultless German without an accent. This is quite remarkable since the Hungarians I have known have all had strong accents. The principal language of the Empire was German since the seat of the government was in Vienna, and anyone who wanted to get ahead learned it at an early age. I believe that my maternal grandmother was born in Slovakia, at the time also part of the Empire.

"Are you ready?" Mother called. "We are off to the market."

It was mid-morning. Mother wore a dirndl-like dress made of a cotton print in red and white squares, and I wore leather shorts and a blue shirt. It was spring and the sun was shining, making it a pleasant day for walking and shopping in the outdoor market just a few blocks from the house. Mother carried her wicker shopping basket. I was between four and five years old and not yet in school. Accompanying Mother to the market was a regular activity for me before I began school at age six. The market was much like a "farmers market" in the United States cities except that this one was quite large — at least it seemed to me at the time. The stalls were staffed by one to three persons, mostly young people. They called out to prospective customers, praising their wares in exaggerated terms.

"Beautiful potatoes, fresh from the farm!"

"Fresh vegetables, straight from the garden: tomatoes, cucumbers, string beans — the best quality!"

I particularly remember a small stall staffed by a pair of buxom women who promoted their wares in loud voices:

"Patchouli, patchouli!" The sound penetrated my ear and seemed to lodge there.

For some years I did not know what this referred to. Finally, I asked Mother:

"What is 'patchouli'"?

"It is an herbal scent, blossoms that have a good, strong smell. People put the blossoms in drawers where they keep clothes and linen to make them smell good."

I was pleased to get this explanation and to finally have the puzzle of this strange-sounding word resolved.

"Buy some spinach," I said to Mother. "I liked the spinach you made a few days ago. What does spinach look like when you buy it? I am never sure what the vegetables look like before you cook them."

"Here it is," Mother replied, chuckling while she pointed to the spinach at a vegetable stall.

Our schools were quite near to our house, and my older sister, Herta, and I walked together most of the way, hers being only a short block away from mine.

It seemed a challenging distance at the time, but when I returned as a grownup, the whole area seemed to have shrunk. School began at 8:00 a.m. and let out at noon for the first four years of primary school. After that, I got out at 1:00 p.m.

As I returned home at noon that day, I climbed the steep stairs, which required a determined effort at the time. A dog's bark announced me. When I arrived on the first floor (one up from the street), I rang, and the maid, Marie, admitted me. I entered the apartment, took a moment to admire the vigor of the waiting dog's wagging tail, gave her a pat on the back and ran into the kitchen.

"Mutti, what did you make for lunch?" I called out while Mother bent down to hug me and kiss me on the cheek. "The smells here are good! I am hungry. Oh, you are making *Beuschel mit Knödel* (innards with dumplings). Great!"

This was a favorite dish of mine on the list of regulars.

"You will have to wait for Herta to come home," was Mother's reply, "just be patient and don't make a fuss," she continued, hugging me again briefly for reassurance.

Mother and the maid wore aprons over their dresses while cooking. I grumbled some while hanging out in the kitchen and watching, but had learned to keep myself in check. Mother did not look kindly on my complaining too much or throwing a fit as I had done sometimes. It had been my experience that she could punish me and banish me from the lunch table if I misbehaved. There were definitely limits to her tolerance. Herta eventually arrived, and we sat down for lunch. I savored the sauce, which was a bit vinegary.

Our diet was strong on starches — macaroni and cheese, boiled and sliced potatoes in a dill sauce, *risi-bisi* (a dish of rice and peas), and creamed spinach topped with a fried egg, sunny-side-up — were part of the regular fare. Salads were thinly sliced cucumbers or butter lettuce topped with an oil-and-vinegar dressing. String beans, cauliflower, and carrots were standard vegetables served in cream sauces.

Father never was home for lunch, which was our main meal of the day. He arrived at about 2:30 p.m., when there were often already some patients in the waiting room who had been admitted by the maid. He ate his lunch in snatches of time between seeing patients during his surgery hours of 3:00 p.m. and

5:00 p.m. When his meal was prepared, he was informed of its being ready by a knock on his surgery door located next to the living/dining room. He was not always free to come out, and often the lunch had to be reheated multiple times before he could finally manage to eat it. Then he would complain loudly and bitterly about the taste, which, according to Mother, had deteriorated because of this process. Only on Sundays did we have lunch as a complete family.

The muffled booms came at regular intervals. For the past two days I had seen army convoys moving up the street consisting of trucks towing what seemed like large guns and others carrying soldiers. It was February 1934 and I was eight years old. I had also seen from our window policemen walking in pairs wearing steel helmets with rifles slung over their shoulders. This was unusual. Normally, policemen walked the streets singly, wore uniform caps and did not have rifles. This scenario and the booms aroused in me an element of excitement spiced with some underlying fear. I felt both excited and threatened. I had not yet accepted that these two feelings can coexist, that fear or risk can enhance excitement, like when I rode my bicycle unsteadily and finally fell over but wanted to get up and try again.

"What is going on?" I asked Mother.

"The soldiers and guns are moving towards Floridsdorf where there are large workers' housing compounds like the *Karl-Marx-Hof*; many workers live in this district. I think that these workers have resisted attempts by the Government-supported militia, the *Heimwehr* (Homeguard) to disarm them. Better ask Father when he comes home. We have to stay indoors for now. It may be dangerous to leave the house."

Herta and I had, in fact, stayed home from school that morning. It was as if everybody was waiting, but for what I did not know.

"What is a militia?" I asked.

"It is a group of soldiers, but not quite the army," Mother added.

It was confusing to me at the time and this was not surprising. It turns out that the government, headed by the chancellor Engelbert Dollfuss, the leader of the Christian Socialist Party, supported a militia and the Social Democrats or workers' party, the opposition in the Parliament, had another militia, called *Schutzbund* (Protective Organization). In addition, there was the national army. It appears that the government wanted to suppress the Social Democrats and sent its party's militia to disarm the other militia. The latter resisted, and fighting between the two militias broke out. Then the government turned out the army to finish the job. The army artillery bombarded the workers' compounds, where the Social Democrats were entrenched, and crushed the rebellion. Similar fights broke out in other cities. A parallel situation in the United States would have had the Republicans and the Democrats each having a militia and the President sending his militia and the army to defeat the militia of the opposition. I do not dare to proceed further with this illustrative analogy.

When Father returned home, I did not obtain any significant further clarification. How do you explain this complex situation to an eight year old? He did, however, repeat Mother's admonition to stay indoors. We were at some distance from the fight, but nobody knew in which direction and how far the unrest might spread. After a few days — three or four — the guns fell silent and the situation, as far as we were concerned, had returned to its previous state of stability — or more accurately, instability.

Otto Schnepp

The Social Democrats suffered nearly 200 dead and over 300 wounded while the police and army suffered 128 deaths and 409 wounded, according to the sources I found on the Internet. Several leaders of the protest movement were executed, and a few succeeded in fleeing the country. In the aftermath of the uprising, the Social Democratic Party, trade unions and all representative bodies led by the Social Democrats on the municipal and provincial levels were banned. A new Constitution of May 1934 was declared, establishing a "corporate state." The Parliament, for all intents and purposes, became inoperative. In other words, Austria became a Fascist state under Dollfuss's one-party leadership. It appears that the government had planned to suppress the opposition, and the latter fell into the trap and resisted forcefully enough to give Dollfuss the cover for the eradication of the opposition.

The next incident started for me at the swimming pool. It was a warm summer day during the two months of summer vacation and the two weeks of the year when it was really hot.

Mother had brought sandwiches and we ate our lunch on the lawn. The loudspeaker played music, and once an hour it announced some news, which did not interest me, and I did not understand in any case.

There was a strict rule governing our return to the pool after eating.

"Remember, you must not go back into the water for half an hour after eating!" Mother admonished.

Then, about an hour later, the loudspeaker suddenly interrupted the music and blared: "*Achtung* (Attention). There has been an attack on the Chancery on Ballhausplatz. The Chancellor Dollfuss and others are being held prisoner inside the Chancery and the attackers don't allow anyone to approach. The fate of these hostages is unknown. We will bring more news as we watch the development of this story."

I did not understand the announcement — some of the words were not even in my vocabulary. I had heard the name Dollfuss mentioned by my parents during the February uprisings. But I understood that something important had happened from the reaction of the people at the pool. I saw groups of grownups talking excitedly, and I wanted to know what was going on. Who was fighting with whom this time? I had already lived through one crisis in February of that year and considered myself experienced in such matters. Mother made an effort to explain something, but she also didn't know what had happened. It was overwhelming and beyond the realm of possibility to think that the seat of the country's government had been attacked and occupied and that the head of state and other officials were being held prisoner.

Much later, I came to understand that the impossible had in fact happened. An underground troop of the Nazi SA had planned and executed an attack on the Chancery using a rented truck and wearing some uniforms that resembled ones worn by the Austrian army. This ragtag group drove into the Chancery without being challenged by the guards at the gate and stormed into the building. One of them shot Dollfuss, and he bled to death while the attackers held off the police and army. They actually had planned to take the entire Cabinet hostage and then take over the country. This did not happen because the government received a warning, which nobody believed was for real but just to be sure, most Ministers were asked to leave the Chancery. Nobody thought it worthwhile to order the gates closed! So much for the famous Austrian virtue *Gemütlichkeit* (relaxed attitude). Eventually, the Nazis surrendered when troops finally showed up and the affair ended. But the head of the government, Chancellor Engelbert Dollfuss, was dead.

It could be concluded from this event that Austria was vulnerable and security even for the highest officials was inadequate. Dollfuss had outlived the establishment of the one-party rule with power concentrated in his hands by barely two months. Austria was not to remain independent for much longer. In March 1938, Hitler's Germany occupied and annexed it.

Chapter 2

Musical
Experiences

"Mutti, Walter said that he has gone to see an opera at the Staatsoper. The tickets for the standing section are cheap. I want to go with him. He says that he wants to go next Saturday to see an opera called *Der Rosenkavalier*. It is by Strauss. Can I go with him?"

"I will talk to Papa. Yes, I want you to go. This will be a good experience. But, you know, this is not the Johann Strauss who composed the *Fledermaus* (The Bat) that you have heard on the radio on New Year's Eve and you liked to march across the room reciting: '*Die Fledermaus von Johann Strauss.*' It is Richard Strauss who composed the *Rosenkavalier*."

"Great, I will tell Walter, and he will help me buy the ticket. We can walk to the *Staatsoper* (State Opera House) across the Inner City. I can pick him up on the way; he lives in the 9th District."

I was 11 years old, and Walter attended the same *gymnasium* (high school) in Vienna near where we lived on *Wallensteinplatz*. I had an inkling that Mother would support me in spite of the constant concern about money that I frequently heard in my parents' conversations. Culture was important to both my parents, but particularly to Mother. On Saturday, Mother gave me the money I needed and Walter and I set out on this adventure. We walked from Walter's house to the *Stephansplatz* where the big St. Stephen's cathedral is located and then down the *Kärntnerstrasse* to the Opera House. The large opera house, the crowds of people and then the music, all added to the excitement. When the curtain went up on the richly appointed stage, the singers appeared and the performance began. I understood many of the words since the libretto for this opera is in German with quite a bit of Viennese slang thrown in, although the singing distorted the words and made it difficult for me to understand some of it. When we walked home, I felt very grown up and had a sense of achievement. It was as if I had advanced a notch toward becoming an adult.

We had a grand piano in the living room of our apartment and Mother played occasionally. My sister, Herta, three years older than I, had studied piano for two years with a woman-teacher who had taught Mother. Herta practiced her music assignments at home, and I had become accustomed to hearing music in the house as well as on the radio. Also my father had had some musical education playing the violin, although Mother considered his achievement to be on a lower level than hers, as I understood from remarks she dropped here and there. When I turned ten, it was my turn to be sent to study piano with the same teacher. I was not really enthusiastic, but I accepted the idea that music was a legitimate part of education.

It was a rainy Sunday afternoon in the fall, and this was a rare occasion: all four of us were at home, even Father, who was usually busy at any time, even on weekends, with his medical practice: working at some hospital clinic, making house calls or seeing patients in his clinic which was part of our apartment. My sister and I were reading or doing home-work.

"Wow! We are going to hear a concert!" Herta ex-claimed.

Indeed, Mother had sat down at the piano, and Father was in the process of opening his violin case after extracting it from the storage place where it lay, forgotten, most of the time.

"This is a beautiful piece by Beethoven," Herta commented for my benefit as the two of us sat on the couch, listening. "We are lucky to have a musical atmosphere at home. Not all of my friends have parents who are that well-educated."

For me, Herta was a model that I wanted to emu-late, and I certainly accepted her judgment. My sense of myself was therefore also enhanced, alt-hough I doubt that I would have expressed this in such lofty terms at the time.

"I wish they would play more often," Herta con-tinued in a whisper. "I really enjoy music. Mother quite often plays by herself, but when they play to-gether, it is something special!"

When I had studied the piano for ten months, our teacher announced that she planned a recital by her students before an audience composed mostly of families and friends. The program was announced, and we were all busy preparing our parts. To my surprise, I was also to participate. I felt some fear of playing in public, no matter how friendly the audience.

"Don't worry. You will do fine," the teacher assured me.

Mother promised to help me practice, or rather to supervise me and make sure that I kept at it. I also had the example of my sister, who worked at her part assiduously. All this attention got to me, and I decided to be diligent. I cooperated fully and practiced almost every day. In preparation for the great event, my mother planned to make a silk shirt for me. She bought a *Resterl* or a remainder piece of material of a bolt at her favorite piece goods store on *Wallensteinstrasse*, and she worked this project in with other plans for clothes for herself and for us children. The house seamstress came for a few days, and Mother worked with her. They used Mother's treadle Singer sewing machine, which intrigued me. I liked to watch how the material was guided by their nimble fingers under the sewing machine's foot and came out stitched so evenly. Eventually, I was a nuisance, and Mother shooed me away.

"Go and find something else to do. You are getting in our way," she said, and her tone expressed annoyance.

After a fitting and some finishing touches, the new shirt was ready. It even had cuffs and Mother got me some cufflinks made of woven cord of the same off-white color. This was something new for me, and I learned to insert them, although at first I needed help from Herta or Mother. I felt quite grown-up when I was allowed to wear it for a few minutes at a time just to get acquainted with it.

The day of the student concert arrived and Herta, Mother and I prepared to leave the house for the performance hall. Father, to nobody's surprise was not available. Herta carried her music score under her arm but I went without.

"Won't you take your music with you?" Herta asked me.

"No," I responded. "I have played the piece so often — I know it well."

Looking back, I now marvel at my self-assurance at the time. But soon I was to regret my bravado.

After we arrived, and while just waiting around for the concert to begin, I tried to imagine myself placing my hands on the keyboard. I just could not remember how I would begin my piece.

"Oh, how I long to have my music with me," I told Herta who was waiting in the same room with all the other student performers. To top it off, I was the first performer on the program. How I was selected was not explained to me. I was the youngest in age and also had studied for the shortest time!

"When you sit down at the piano, it will all come back to you," Herta comforted me. To her credit, she did not say, "I told you to take your music."

The time came, and I had to go on stage and face all these people. I took a bow as the audience applauded. I sat down at the piano, and did not know how to begin! And, it did not all come back to me, as Herta had promised. I played a few notes and stopped. I repeated this sequence several times. The tension in the room was palpable; at least I knew for sure that I was tense. My hands were clammy, and I began to feel terror. I believed that everybody realized that I was stuck. Finally, I decided to move forward, no matter what I came up with. I improvised the beginning part, which had to be repeated several times. Somehow I figured out how to play something approaching the real piece. It did not sound quite right — it was a bit dissonant. It was more like a piece of modern music, as I would characterize it now, instead of the melodious original. I heard a big sigh of relief rising from the audience. I realized then that I had been right — they all understood what was going on, but they were on my side. I repeated my original composition several times as called for, and finally, finally I finished. I got a big round of enthusiastic applause! I bowed to the audience and fled the stage.

Of course, Herta performed flawlessly, according to the family chatter, but the rest of the concert was all a blur to me. To my surprise, nobody was mad at me — not the teacher, not Mother, not Herta, and not even my uncle Gyuri who had arrived in time to hear me. In fact they all complimented me on my handling of my dilemma. That was my first — and last — concert performance.

A year or so later, in March 1938, the Nazi German annexation of Austria ended all musical aspirations in our family. My having to give up the piano was not any great loss to society, but Herta did have some talent, Mother thought. The grand piano was sold for a pittance before we had to give up our apartment and move in with my grandmother. Soon thereafter, all four of us fled the country, Herta to Kenya in East Africa and my parents and I to Shanghai. I did not see my sister again until 1952, fourteen years later.

I did acquire some lasting basic knowledge of music in the short course of my studies, and to this day, some 75 years later, I enjoy concerts. In fact, the incentive to write this piece originated from recently attending a concert of the San Francisco Symphony Orchestra. As I watched a pianist perform, I was reminded of my childhood experience.

Chapter 3

Under Nazi Rule

The events I describe in this chapter are my own experiences, as I remember them. I believe the account is quite accurate except for some details of the dialogue. The events all took place in Vienna after the annexation of Austria by Germany in March 1938 and before my emigration to Shanghai in late January 1939. Shanghai was chosen as a refuge by approximately 20,000 Jews from Germany, Austria and Poland because it was at that time the only place in the world where people without means could immigrate without the requirement of a visa. This was so because Shanghai was, in part, an international city and not part of any country.

In view of the fact that Germany invaded Poland, triggering the outbreak of WWII on September 1st 1939, it may seem that my parents and I left Nazi

Germany in the nick of time. It all happened in less than one year. There just was not much time to make decisions to uproot lives, raise the means necessary for fares — the voyage to Shanghai took four weeks and was commensurately expensive — and to complete all necessary formalities. And this is not to speak of the courage and determination it took to go to foreign and distant shores, facing a future devoid of certainty. I turned 13 in July 1938 and did not confront the question of survival, but my parents certainly must have faced that question. It is to my father's credit that he pushed for our leaving with great energy and he had the foresight to understand that the danger to our survival was even greater if we were to remain in Vienna. As it turned out, my father's judgment proved accurate, and I am indebted to his wisdom for my survival.

The annexation of Austria by Nazi Germany marked a major break in my young life and was the source of deep-felt trauma, which burdened my psychological development for several decades. My memoirs chronicle the sources of this trauma and the path I chose in my attempt to overcome it and to return to being a fully human and feeling person. I consider this process to have been one of the major achievements of my life.

The shrill ring of the doorbell cut through the calm of the apartment, followed by several more jarring bursts. The maid opened the front door, and three men in civilian clothes burst in unceremoniously.

One of them called out in a loud voice, "Is the man at home?"

The maid replied, "No, he is not at home. Only the mistress is here." Her voice had a slight quiver and signaled uncertainty and discomfort — perhaps even some fear.

"Where is he?" the intruder shot back.

"Probably at work" was the response; her voice had steadied and conveyed a trace of resistance.

I was in that apartment visiting a school friend, as I had often done before. We were 12 years old, going on 13. I was aware that these people must be Nazi officials, probably of the feared GESTAPO.

They took charge of the apartment and one of them said to the maid in Viennese dialect and in a commanding tone, "You and I will wait downstairs in the car for the man of the house to return. You will point him out to me when he comes."

Otto Schnepp

The maid made no response. She seemed to have decided to bow to the Nazi's order. The other two strangers took command of the premises. The parents of my friend were Jewish while the maid obviously was not. I was in a state of shock and did not know what to do. I was uncertain if I could sit down but was afraid to ask. Play was out of the question. Both of us boys stood around as if paralyzed, barely making any move and instinctively avoided attracting attention. None of us spoke. My friend's mother was somewhere, but she showed no sign of her presence. I imagined that she was in a back room being questioned, but I heard only some murmurs.

My mind was racing, posing questions to which I had no answers. What was happening? What would become of me? Would they take me away, as I knew they had done to many Jewish men in those days of spring 1938, following the *Anschluss* (annexation) of Austria to Nazi Germany? True, in all instances I had heard of, the men were grownups. But who knew? I had witnessed the Viennese welcoming the German troops with enthusiasm in March 1938, and later, when Hitler visited, he was greeted as a liberator. Jews, by edict and by the evidence of cruel and suppressive actions, had been declared an underclass without rights and were now free game, exposed to random arrest and capricious physical attacks. Bands of teenagers could and did attack young boys like me. I had begun to admit to myself that nobody, including my parents, had the power to protect me.

My parents had always thought of themselves as Austrian, and this conviction was a basic part of their personalities. My father had fought in the Austrian army for all four years of WWI and had earned three military decorations with crossed swords on their ribbons, indicating that they had been awarded "for actions of bravery in the face of the enemy." All this past had now been denied and invalidated.

As a child, I had not been taught any of the values of Jewish culture and therefore had no defense against the Nazis' slanderous distortions of the Jewish personality and character. I was vulnerable and open to absorbing the anti-Semitic propaganda freely disbursed by Göbbels, Hitler's Propaganda Minister, and his publication *Der Stürmer*. I felt rudderless, unworthy and confused — and in retrospect, I believe my parents were as well. We all lived in a state of bewilderment and fear. My father seemed to me to be the only one who retained an outside calm and never let on that there was an impending threat hanging over us. This image of steadiness was a source of comfort to me and, I believe, to my mother and my sister as well.

The telephone rang several times, and one of the Nazis answered it: "The telephone is closed."

An hour, perhaps more, must have passed in this state of suspense and fear. Then the doorbell rang again — this time just a single burst followed by silence. One of the men opened the door, and there stood … my 15-year-old sister!

"What do you want?" I heard the man ask.

I was surprised and encouraged by her firm reply, "I have come to take my brother home!"

"Where is he?"

"There" she responded pointing at me. The Nazi was obviously nonplussed.

"Take him away then," I heard him say.

I felt a surge of relief and joy, took my jacket and we marched out. My sister was my heroine of the day! She had come, braved the dragon and rescued me. I felt reassured by the knowledge that there was somebody else beside my father in the family who kept a sense of coolness and dignity.

Chapter 4

Voyage to Shanghai and Our Beginnings There

In January 1939, I departed from Vienna for Shanghai, accompanying the couple with whom my parents had exchanged ship tickets in late November of the year before. I had briefly met them at the train station when my parents left on what was for us, a traumatic evening.

Now a small family group came to see me off including my Aunt Mitzi, her son Gert and my Uncle Gyuri. My grandmother stayed at home; I had already parted from her tearfully. I was a youngster of 13 and was confused about my feelings. I was certainly glad to be on my way to rejoin my parents. However, I was also sad to leave behind the familiar place where I had lived since my birth. I remember my aunt gently scolding me for looking sad as I waved goodbye from the window of the train.

"Don't look so sad, Otto! Be happy to finally be on your way to see your parents again."

The train was to take us on an overnight trip across the Alps to Genoa in Italy where we were to embark on the ocean liner *Conte Biancamano* of the Lloyd Triestino shipping line that would take us all the way to Shanghai, a four-week voyage. As the train approached the Italian border, we got our documents ready for inspection. I experienced a few minutes of panic because I could not locate the tax document I needed to show. To my relief, I finally found it.

An SS man in a black uniform came through to check the passengers' documents. As he came to us, he recognized Mr. Just, the man I was traveling with.

"I remember you from when you were in *Schutzhaft* (protective custody)," he said. This was their euphemism for their imprisonment of Jews to coerce transfer of property or just to torture them.

After the SS man had left, Mr. Just confirmed that he also recognized the SS man. The encounter led to

Mr. Just's recalling some of his experiences during his arrest. He told of their being ordered to hold up their hands and guards stripping off their wedding and other rings. He also recounted that they were given classifications, and some received the letter F. These men were taken to another room from which the other prisoners heard cries of pain, and they thus assumed that F stood for *Folter* or torture. I recall listening to his stories with some dread as the reality of the threat I had also felt during those weeks and months in Vienna settled in again. I then felt immense relief when we finally crossed the border and left Germany behind.

In Genoa, we stayed one night at a small hotel. Mr. Just taught me two words in Italian: *kiave trentotto* or "key 38" (my room number), in order to recover the key from the reception desk.

On the ship, I was quartered in a third class cabin that I shared with three women, including the woman with whom I was travelling. The steward who served us meals spoke broken English. Sometimes he brought some dishes from the *fershta classa* (First Class). We often saw another higher level crewmember who spoke in equally broken German.

Otto Schnepp

We passed through the Suez Canal, and on the banks I saw my first camel outside a zoo. I remember it well — it was an impressive sight silhouetted against a clear blue sky. We were not welcome to go ashore in every port where the ship anchored. I assume that they did not want to have several hundred poor refugees flood in who were not good prospects for making purchases, but I never found out what these decisions were really based on.

Most of the time, we had good weather and calm seas, but we also encountered storms on the way. I was seasick at these times, and in those days, there was no Dramamine to help. I could not stand up, but I never threw up. I just had to keep still, and then I was alright. Some grownups took pity on me and helped me find a place on deck, and the fresh air was also refreshing. People said I should eat to feel better, but I could not move.

At one point a male crewmember approached me and said: "Come with me to play," pointing to the stairs that led to the cabins and, I assumed, also to the crew's quarters. I considered how to react and had some curiosity about finding out what he meant. Fortunately some other passenger overheard the conversation and intervened energetically.

"Geh weg und lass diesen Burschen in Ruh! (Go away and leave this youngster alone!)"

I doubt that the crewmember understood the words spoken in German, but the tone and gestures that accompanied them made the intention abundantly clear, and he quickly disappeared down the stairs.

One scene made an impression on me, and I remember it clearly. At some point, an Indian man came on board and stayed for a stretch of the voyage. It should be said that in third class, there were no individual bathrooms attached to cabins, and baths were in shared facilities, but could be reserved. I overheard a group of women passengers, who were all Jewish refugees, discussing the implications of the presence of the Indian.

"Now this Indian will take a bath in the same bathtub that I may use! Imagine that," one of the women said, and the others agreed that this possibility presented a serious problem.

Although I was only 13 years old, I realized that this expression of racial discrimination was, under the circumstances, entirely ludicrous. Here we all were refugees from racial discrimination of the worst kind, and yet these women were concerned about the threat of an Indian man bathing in the same tub! This experience taught me how deeply ingrained racial discrimination and fear of mingling with persons of color was among the population of central Europe.

The ship anchored in Colombo, then the capital of Ceylon, the island just south of the Indian peninsula, which is now called Sri Lanka, and we were allowed ashore. As I left the ship with my guardians, a kind elderly local with a white beard approached us.

"May I offer you and your son some drinks?" he inquired in English while looking at me. "I would like to do a kindness to the young boy," he added. All of us understood the question, and the couple quickly consented. They did not explain that I was not their son.

The man led us to a near-by drink bar, and I recall getting lemonade served in a tall glass. The drink was delicious, and I sipped it happily from a straw. There was something luxurious about this drink, and it obviously made a deep impression on me. After all, this happened 75 years ago and I still remember the experience clearly.

Back onboard, we encountered a final storm, a cyclone they called it in the announcement over the

PA system, between Manila and Hong Kong, and I experienced another bout of seasickness. We then sailed north through calm seas sheltered by the Chinese mainland coast to Shanghai. Shanghai does not lie on the oceanfront but is accessed by way of the Huangpu River, one of the waterways comprising the delta of the Yangtse River. The ship anchored offshore, and boats took us to the customhouse on the Bund, the riverside road in the International Settlement. The customs officers were all British. I had my passport ready for inspection but to my surprise, nobody asked for it. The customs officers were only interested in the baggage, and then I saw my parents waiting for me! This was a deeply emotional moment for all of us. I hugged my mother and we both shed tears of joy. I must also have hugged Father, but I do not recall how I greeted him. He was mainly a well-controlled man, although I had seen tears in his eyes when my parents left me behind in Vienna.

My parents lived in a single room in a ramshackle house in the French Concession, sharing a bathroom and kitchen with other renters. The French Concession bordered seamlessly on the International Settlement, but the streets changed names as one passed the border. For example, Seymour Road be-

Greek — not much use in the present world. Mother introduced me to the lady, and I gathered that she had spoken to her before.

"Well, I will try to find a good home for Otto," the lady began and added, "There are many families in the Russian Jewish community who are willing to take in refugee children."

This pronouncement hit me in my belly. Here I had been separated from my parents for two and a half months and had looked forward to finally being reunited with them. And now I understood that this lady was looking for a family to take me in and to separate us once more. A tsunami wave of anguish broke over me, and I wept uncontrollably. Fortunately, my mother grasped the source of my grief immediately, quickly back-pedaled on the plan to place me with another family and it was never mentioned again. I later understood that long-term residents, mostly members of the Russian Jewish community, took in a number of refugee youngsters to offer them a more comfortable home than their parents were able to afford.

The next day my mother took me to the Shanghai Jewish School, which was about a ten-minute walk from our place, and I was duly registered. This school was supported by the Jewish community and followed a syllabus modeled on the English educational system. I was interviewed by Mr. Kahan, a senior teacher, who determined that I was advanced enough in algebra to be placed in a class designated as "Upper Five." The teachers at this school were all recruited from the local English-speaking Jewish communities except for the teacher of English language and literature, who was hired from England. Her name was O'Dwyer. There were four other refugee students in this class and Mrs. O'Dwyer referred to us collectively as "the German children." I was the youngest student in the class. In the school there were probably more than fifty refugee students spread over a variety of classes, most of whom were bussed in from the area called Hongkew (Hong Kou in Mandarin), a distance of about half an hour's travel.

Everything was strange to me including the language of instruction. During the first two weeks, I understood very little, which understates the situation — I actually understood next to nothing that was said. The other "German children" tried to keep me informed about what was going on, and that helped me. All this difficulty was resolved within a few weeks, my English improved and I could then stand on my own two feet. For quite a while, I needed to ask for explanations at times, but the trauma of living in a bubble separate from my environment was over, and from then on I made steady progress and soon placed within the first three or four scholastically in a class of 30. I do remember studying the geography of Canada by learning whole paragraphs from the book by heart because I did not have the vocabulary to recount the content in my own words. I should mention that I had studied English as a foreign language for a year in school in Vienna, and Father magically produced a private teacher with whom all three of us — Father, my sister and I — studied more intensively for a few months. But none of these efforts was enough to prevent my living for a few weeks in a bubble separate from my fellow students and teachers.

On September 3rd 1939, Britain and France declared war on Germany following the latter's invasion of Poland. Mrs. O'Dwyer explained that this situation presented a problem since we, the "German children," now belonged to a country that was at war with the countries of the "others." All this was quite vague, and internally, I rebelled against her stated position. I assumed that, along with me all other refugee students understood that we had been declared an underclass expelled from Germany and did not want to be labeled "German" and therefore enemies in Shanghai. I stewed over this issue, but was not capable of protesting Mrs. O'Dwyer's position. I did not yet feel sufficiently secure in my knowledge of English to argue the case, and also her authority as a teacher intimidated me in a system that was still new and unfamiliar to me. I did raise the issue with the other refugee students and got support from all but one. To my surprise and horror, one of them argued that the victorious Allies had maltreated Germany and Austria after WWI and the Germans were justified in wanting to seek revenge and to recover their prominence. I knew of this argument, since it had been used by Hitler, and I was amazed to learn that a Jewish refugee from Nazi Germany would defend the Nazi aggression after anti-Semitism had been adopted as official German government policy. From the information I had obtained from my parents, it was clear to me that we all, and in particular Jews, would be threatened if Germany were to prevail.

Life soon became routine, and we adjusted as well as we could. My father, a physician, had opened a medical office downtown with the help of committees set up by long-term Jewish residents, but his income could barely support our low level of existence. For myself, I progressed in school and soon began to read a lot using the school library. I joined the Boy Scout troop attached to the school and made some friends.

Here is a short description of the Jewish communities in Shanghai. As everywhere in the world, there were two large groupings of Jews. The Sephardic community originated mainly in Iraq and included some who had obtained British subject status, presumably from living in India as traders. Some Sephardic Jews were prominent and wealthy: Sir Victor Sassoon, who owned a great deal of the real estate in the International Settlement of Shanghai, and Sir Ellie Kadoorie are examples. Then there was the more numerous Ashkenazi community, whose members had come to the northeastern part of China, called Manchuria, to escape anti-Semitic pogroms in Tsarist Russia. There was a large community in Harbin, a Russian cultural and trading center. They then transferred to Shanghai, where

Chapter 5

Shanghai After Pearl Harbor

In school, final examinations were scheduled for the first two weeks of December 1941. These were administered by local trustees for the Cambridge-Oxford Overseas Examination Syndicate and were to be sent to England for evaluation. Because there was already war between Britain and France on one hand and Germany on the other, precautions were taken in that we wrote the examinations in duplicate to ensure safe delivery.

The Japanese attack on Pearl Harbor on December 7 and the outbreak of war in the Pacific had important consequences for us. The Japanese army occupied the International Settlement of Shanghai during the night of that day and erected barriers on the streets as a means of controlling the city. Procedures were worked out to allow us to complete the examinations but there was great uncertainty as to what the immediate consequences of the Japanese takeover would be.

At first I had no idea how the outbreak of the war in the Pacific would affect my life. My father's income shrank significantly as all sectors of the local population faced uncertainty. My own modest moneymaking activities also screeched to a halt. In addition, I now had nothing to do since the local job opportunities evaporated in the face of the crisis. I had never been sure just what I would do after completing school, and had only had vague ideas of getting a job with some company, then working my way up. For a long time my own ambition had been to study medicine, but in our financial situation — even before Pearl Harbor — university studies were out of the question.

We did manage to survive, I do not really know how. I somehow found the money to buy a book entitled *Science for the Citizen* and I immersed myself in the study of the history of the measurement of time and the intricacies of the calendar. Also, I was able to join the library of the local *Alliance Francaise* and read books in French, advancing my knowledge of that language significantly. I remember eventually being able to read books by Balzac after a month or two, and I enjoyed both their content as well as the idea of my being able to read and understand them in the original. I spent many hours reading in Jessfield Park (now *Zhongshan Gongyuan* or Sun Yat-Sen Park) near where I lived when the weather was fair. I was, however, very lonely most of the time because the one friend I had was still attending school.

As already mentioned, the family's financial situation was even more precarious during the period following Pearl Harbor than it had been before, until I began earning some money a few months later. Our hand-to-mouth subsistence depended on my father's earnings, which were meager and unreliable. Several times we actually had no money to buy food and no stores to draw on. Plainly put, we went hungry. Mother expressed her distress openly and complained of pain caused by hunger. For me it was more painful to hear her complaints than the experience of hunger itself. My immediate reaction was anger at Mother, which in retrospect I interpret as covering my guilt at not being able to provide for her. These feelings, I hypothesize, were driven by my having accepted responsibility for my mother's well-being — I had begun to play a parental role towards her. I suspect that I had accepted the role of protector, which my mother encouraged in me, and I further believe that in later life I broadened this attitude to include all women with whom I had close relations. The role of "daddy" has colored all my relationships with women and I have not given it up completely even to this day. In fact, I consider my awareness of this neurosis and of its effects on my life a significant step in my emotional development.

Twice my father decided on a desperate measure. He sent me to sell some of his most cherished belongings — his medical books. He directed me to take the books to a certain store which was located in the Sassoon House, where his office was and which he obviously knew well. I have a painfully clear memory of the first such trip to town. I recall the suitcase in which I carried the books, the English-style double-decker bus I took, my sitting on the top level and the views I had of the estates that lined the route. I was quite anxious about my mission and I pondered some questions: would the bookstore actually be willing to buy the books or would they send me away, rejected and defeated? My anxiety was heightened by the awareness that my failure to sell the books would also bring with it failure to provide us with several days of sustenance and failure to bring back the means to buy food for my suffering mother! The stakes seemed high.

Actually, my mission was crowned with success. The owner came out to inspect the books and quoted a price to which I readily agreed. I do not recall the sum or purchasing power of the proceeds but I returned triumphantly and mother went to buy some supplies. The immediate result was that we ate kippered herring from cans that must have been left over from imported stocks before Pearl Harbor. The second time I was sent on a similar mission, I was more prepared and more confident of success. The result was similar to the first sales trip, even to the kippered herrings we ate to satisfy our hunger.

(As I wrote these paragraphs I relived the described experiences and the attached emotions — pain, sadness and some shame for having been so degraded and defeated by circumstances that I was as yet powerless to fight against. Writing this last sentence brought on a rush of sadness and fear. The vagaries of life still threaten my sense of security and the imprint of these memories still has the power to challenge my confidence in my survival capability, which usually has the upper hand.)

For me as a refugee, life in Shanghai after Pearl Harbor under Japanese occupation was limited and devoid of hope for the future. We were just hanging on and living from one day to the next. Our lives were in suspense. I was 18 in 1943 when we were forced to move into the "designated area." The community organized cultural and social activities to encourage the dispirited refugees.

Fortunately for me, I was not dependent on life in the district. I spent almost all my days outside at the university or tutoring to earn a living. I returned home at night and usually hung around on Sunday mornings. The intellectual stimulation and challenges of my studies kept me busy, and my tutoring, which occupied between 30 to 40 hours per week, did not allow my participation in any of the community-based activities. This crowded schedule also helped me to live in denial about the dangers to which I was exposed. Nevertheless, occasionally the feeling of having been forgotten by the world intruded on my thoughts.

ROOTS LOST-ROOTS FOUND

One day in early 1945, I was sitting on the steps of a lecture hall building at the university with a group of students when we heard a series of short blasts of the siren, indicating an air raid alarm, and shortly thereafter a burst of gunfire assaulted my ears.

"Air raid! Air raid!"

The calls came from many places on campus. We all took shelter inside the buildings. I stayed close to the entrance and looked out occasionally to see what was going on. I soon heard the whirring of high-flying planes and then a series of dull thuds, which I interpreted to be the explosions of bombs dropped at some distance. Bursts of loud gunfire, presumably from a near-by anti-aircraft battery, intermittently shattered the silence. Soon we heard a long siren blast, which was the all-clear signal. This was followed by the louder sound of airplane engines. After several repetitions of this sequence we understood that high-flying U.S. planes were dropping the bombs and Japanese planes only took off after the attackers had gone. According to the joke that circulated, the noise of the Japanese planes was the real all-clear signal.

Otto Schnepp

My reaction to the first air raids was not fear or anger at the attackers. Rather, I was relieved. I expressed my mood to my fellow students:

"Finally something is happening!"

By this time, we knew that the war in Europe had turned in favor of the allied U.S. and British forces, and we certainly celebrated this development. The local Russian radio station reported only on this theater of war. The almost daily triumphant announcements of *Prekass* which we all knew signified a Proclamation of some victory or other, followed by *Krasna Armi*, or Red Army, assured us that the European war was all but over. But, the appearance of the American planes, however hostile their actions seemed on the surface, was an occurrence which I felt as a personal reassurance that we had not been forgotten, and it gave me hope that the endgame was also approaching in our part of the world. Actually, I was right in the crossfire, but danger still seemed to be some distance away. Also, at the age of 19 I lived under the delusion of invulnerability.

After some months of high-level overflights and bombardments at a distance, there was a significant change. One Sunday morning I was in the district at the house of a young woman student who attended the French university, Université L'Aurore, whom I was tutoring in physics. The air raid siren sounded the ominous series of short blasts. We did not intend to interrupt our studies, but my student's father burst in and ordered us to take shelter under the bed. She complied and invited me to join her. I did. Not having any romantic aspect to our relationship we did not have any clear plan as to how to occupy ourselves. We tried to continue reading her physics book but we could not find a comfortable position in the low space under the bed.

Finally, she said: "This is really crazy. I have had the experience of lying in bed with a young man, but lying under the bed is a new experience altogether."

We laughed heartily. But then the scenario changed drastically. We heard the chilling and protracted screaming sound of a diving plane followed by the loud explosion of a released bomb. This sequence was repeated perhaps ten times, and by then, even we were rattled. The suspense, waiting for the bomb's burst, was unnerving. "Will it hit near us this time?" was the frightening thought that waited for resolution. Danger had now come close. Finally the attacking planes were gone, and we heard the distinctive sound of the scrambling Japanese planes.

The attack was over, and relief flooded over me. Still, neither of us admitted to having been scared.

Although the bombardment had started in earnest, I continued in my routine of going to the university and visiting my students. I still did not feel personally threatened. Then came July 17, 1945 — a day all of us refugees remember with dread. That day planes dropped bombs on a target in the vicinity of the district, and some bombs fell inside it, causing major damage to a large building that had been converted into a crowded living space for refugees. Thirty-one were killed and two hundred fifty were injured. I was far away, busy with my routine of studies and tutoring and knew of the raid only as a distant attack on an undetermined target. I had no idea that bombs had fallen close to home. When I returned that evening, I encountered groups of excited people as I walked home from the tram terminus and caught snatches of the conversation:

"Many dead and more wounded!"

"The hospital is full of the wounded."

"Why did they do this to us? It was a cloudy day, and they could not have seen where they bombed!"

"There will be more bombings and we better run to the large shelter when the alarm sounds. They say it is safe there!"

Inside the district, there was a large jail built by the Shanghai Municipal Council that had been constructed like a fortress. The Japanese police authorities had announced that they would open the basement of this building to the public as an air raid shelter.

When I reached home, I was relieved to find my mother there.

She told me: "The bombs fell a few blocks from us and I was really scared. We ran downstairs to our shelter, and after the raid, the news of the damage and of the many dead and wounded spread quickly. Father went to the hospital to help. He thought that his WWI experience would come in useful. You know how he is. He always hurries to be at the center of the action."

Yes, I could understand my father. The raid offered him, as a physician, an opportunity to feel useful. Indeed, he kept busy at the hospital for several days and returned in the evenings in a better mood than I had seen him in for a long time.

Otto Schnepp

The next day I was again at some distance from the district, tutoring a girl of 15, Miriam — my first wife to be,– when the siren announced another raid. The girl's father burst into the room excitedly and ordered us to go downstairs to the basement. For some reason, I resisted and left the house. I started walking in the direction of the designated area although everybody was supposed to be indoors or in shelters where possible. I never understood why nobody interfered with my determined walk in the empty streets. During a raid, all vehicles were supposed to stop and drivers and passengers were to seek shelter. Eventually, the all-clear signal sounded, and I just kept on walking. I assume now that my desire to be close to my parents drove me on. It took me two hours to reach our neighborhood. When I arrived, I learned that this day there had been no damage in our area. I decided to go to view the damage of the day before, and its extent shocked me. To see the destruction was very different from hearing about it.

I toured the bombed neighborhood. There were bodies of Chinese victims of the raid of the day before, at least a hundred, lying in piles on the street. The sight of this number of dead bodies stacked up, as if they were slaughtered animals, sickened me. They had been living beings, and now they were just raw flesh. I felt nauseated. I left the area, but the sight stayed with me as if a photograph had been imprinted on my memory, and it popped up in my mind whenever I was not concentrating on my activities. With time, the image lessened somewhat in intensity, but it is still there, vivid and gruesome, as I write about it. I have rarely mentioned the experience to others. I suspect that I have avoided it in the hope that the memory would fade and eventually go away altogether.

The refugee population was terrified by the raid that had hit inside the district, and every morning crowds gathered near the jail and sat on the pavement to be prepared to take shelter when the alarm sounded. I never saw the inside of this shelter. Fortunately, no more bombs fell inside the designated area where the refugees lived. However, the bombing of the Shanghai area continued right up to the Japanese surrender in August 1945.

Chapter 6

Triumph

"You are wasting your time selling in that store! You should be studying at a university to advance your education."

Mr. Kahan, the principal of the Shanghai Jewish School, was speaking to me emphatically, enunciating every word. I was taken aback and stunned. The subject of my future had come up tangentially as I was explaining my first attempts to study Chinese. The turn of the conversation took me by surprise.

"But I need to earn money to contribute to the family income. My father's medical practice has suffered significantly since the Japanese takeover of Shanghai after Pearl Harbor," I responded.

I was flattered that Mr. Kahan took an interest in my situation. I had been working as the salesman in a men's accessories store for over a year earning a meager salary that was, for my parents and me, an essential income for our survival. My qualifications for getting this job included my knowledge of French and Chinese in addition to English. The store was located in the part of Shanghai called the French Concession, and we had customers who spoke French and Chinese, yet did not speak English.

Mr. Kahan continued. "As you know, the Public Schools of the Shanghai Municipal Council have closed down, and we have a number of students who have transferred to our school and some need help to adjust to our curriculum. I can refer these to you for tutoring, and I am sure you can earn enough to substitute for your present income and allow some time to attend university."

My heart gave a leap at this unexpected possibility to pursue my ambition for higher education. I left Mr. Kahan's house walking on air. My dream had suddenly come within reach.

I returned home that day, feeling high with optimism in the midst of our really miserable circumstances. It was September 1943. Our diet was poor and sometimes inadequate. There was no end in sight in relation to the war in the Pacific. The Japanese occupation kept us isolated from the world, and we had the sinking feeling of having been forgotten. We had some news of the European theater of war by way of a Russian radio station that was allowed to operate since Japan was not at war with Russia until much later but it was limited to reporting news on what was going on in Europe. We all learned the necessary words to follow the events they reported on.

At 18, my wish for life could not be entirely suppressed, but I did not have the luxury of thinking of a future. To make matters worse, the Japanese Military Authorities had issued a "Proclamation" in February forcing all stateless refugees who had arrived in Shanghai after 1937 to move into a "Designated Area" by May 18. My father, as a physician, had obtained permission to delay the move, but we knew that we would have to comply within a short time. Then our movement outside this area would be subject to permission granted by the authorities.

"I have great news," I called out to my parents as I entered our poor attic apartment, and I told them about my conversation with Mr. Kahan. My parents appreciated my joy, and we all got a substantial boost from the news. I then had to decide when and how to tell the manager of the store, Frau Altura, about my plans and to set a time for my leaving the job. This was the principal subject of our discussion that evening.

"I want to leave my job as soon as I can begin my tutoring. Based on Mr. Kahan's promise, this will only take a few weeks."

Father responded: "Yes, do whatever you can to get an education. Unfortunately, I am not in a position to help you. On the contrary, I rely on your help to see us through these hard times. I am glad that you understand the problem, particularly since I don't know what I will be able to earn after moving to Hongkew. Let's see what Frau Altura will say when you tell her," Father added as an afterthought.

I thought it fair to tell the manager as soon as possible.

"I have something to tell you, Frau Altura," I began. "I have an opportunity to enter the university and to earn money tutoring high school students."

I somehow expected her to congratulate me, or at least to understand my excitement over my new-found good fortune. However, her expression was glum and even angry. She broke off our conversation, and I attended to my duties in the store. About an hour later, she sought me out and spoke to me in a tense voice.

"You don't know the history of your father's beginnings here. At the time, I was the secretary to the head of the committee, Mr. Komor, who provided the money for your father to open his office in the Sassoon House. It was I who went to Mr. Komor to get this support. So you better think about that. You owe me for that help. I deserve your consideration. You must take my interest into account!" She spoke angrily and her face was grim.

I was very young and at first intimidated at the onslaught of this guilt trip. However, I felt anger surging up within me, and that emboldened me to respond.

"I don't owe you anything! You have not been particularly kind to me here. In any case, what you did for my father is between you and him. My future is important to me!"

We did not exchange any more words than necessary for the remainder of the day, nor the following day. Tension hung over the store like a cloud threatening to burst. The third day, Frau Altura addressed me again. This time, her expression was friendly and soft. I sensed that she was about to make me an offer.

"I want you to know that I had a talk with the owner. We want to double your salary. Think it over and discuss it with your father."

Well, I was dumbstruck. And this after the owner had told me a few months before — politely but firmly and tinged with contempt — that I could not expect any increase in salary. He had added: "Go and better yourself if you can!"

That evening, Father and I had a talk. I, of course, was firm in my decision to quit my job and enroll at St. John's University, an American Episcopalian missionary-founded institution where English was the teaching language. At the time, there were no Americans there, but the university managed to keep open during the entire period of the war. I expected my father to agree with me and to support my ambition for higher education.

"Well, you know, double your salary would be a great help for us," Father said to my surprise and disappointment.

I felt a stab to my heart and the slow rise of outrage. I felt betrayed. However, I controlled myself and finally responded with some trepidation:

"Let me work on this. I will try to figure out how much I can earn from tutoring. Mr. Lowy told me the other day that he wants to refer to me a group of Chinese who wish to practice English conversation. They meet on Wednesday evenings and Sunday afternoons. That means that I can begin working with them without waiting for me to quit my job."

I let a day pass and just smiled at the manager. If she had asked me where I stood, I would have told her that I was still thinking, but she did not ask. I believe that she felt pretty sure of her position after my father had asked her two months before for an advance on my salary. She knew that we were short of money.

Finally, the next evening I was ready to deal with Father. We sat at the table after dinner.

"I have figured out what I can earn. I believe that I can earn as much as the double salary they have offered. This is my promise to you and Mother," I said firmly.

I am not sure that Father really believed me, but he did not push me any further. I sighed in relief. I had succeeded in holding to my position. I was left with a queasy feeling in my stomach after having been let down by Father, but standing my ground. I hoped that I would be able to keep my promise.

I gave final notice and quit my job. The owner evidently avoided coming to the store during my final weeks there; I never saw him again. Later, Father told me that he had heard how Frau Altura told people of my ingratitude and betrayal. I guess they did really need me after all.

After having had to borrow money from a good friend of mine (I believe the money came from his parents) to pay the required advance on tuition, I began my studies in February 1944. I have always looked back on this episode in my life with pride. I had launched myself on the road to success after having faced down my Father. I did, however, have to pay a price for having made such a significant commitment to myself. Nevertheless, in the long run, I came away unscathed.

Chapter 7

Ghoya and the Pass

fter our move to the "Designated Area," a euphemism for the Ghetto established by the Japanese military authorities, I had to apply for a pass to allow me to leave this district and to be able to continue my studies at St. John's University and also to attend to my tutoring. This work gave me a modest income to support myself and my parents. My father's earnings had been greatly diminished since he was now limited to occasional consultations within the designated district. The official who authorized these passes was a Japanese man of small stature by the name of Ghoya.

After submitting an application, my name was published on a board outside the police station where the offices of the Shanghai Stateless Refugees Affairs Bureau was located. This was the signal for me to appear before Mr. Ghoya. I went there the next day hoping for the best, but I was frightened. I had heard of people being cursed and slapped in the face on such occasions. Ghoya was known to act out and one story I had heard about occurred when a tall applicant for a pass stood before him. Suddenly, the official, who was short even by Japanese standards, was supposed to have jumped up, stood on his chair and stepped up onto his desk.

"You think you are tall. I can be just as tall — even taller than you!" Ghoya was told to have shouted out, waving his arms.

As I stood in line before entering Ghoya's office, I heard the loud voice of a refugee aide shouting out questions and commands to applicants in German, using a mechanical voice, devoid of any human feeling.

"Where will you work?" "Who is your employer?" "What will be your work there?"

In between the refugee aide's exclamations, some of the same questions in strongly accented English floated to my ear. I presumed this to be the voice of Mr. Ghoya, the self-styled "King of the Jews." Tension was in the air. As I looked at my co-applicants, I saw their strained expressions and knew that I was not the only one who felt anxious. When I was near enough to the door of the office, I could see the "King" sitting at his desk. I fervently hoped that Ghoya would not be incited to torment me.

"Student, St, John's University" he mumbled when my turn came, and that was it.

I breathed a sigh of relief as I took my pass and left, walking faster than usual. With the pass there also came a badge, bearing the Chinese character for "tong" or "pass" in black on a blue background, which I was to wear on my lapel when outside the district.

It was a long way from the district to St. John's University, involving two changes of bus and tram, and it took approximately one hour each way. I was outside the district almost every day for most of the day, either at the university or tutoring students at their homes. Public transportation cost money, and I had to save wherever I could. Also, the public transportation system left much to be desired during the war years and I wound up doing a lot of walking. This was fine much of the time, but when it rained, I often was uncomfortably wet, particularly on winter days since I did not possess a raincoat or an umbrella. My pass allowed me to leave at 8:00 a.m., and I had to be back in the district by 8:00 p.m.

In the evenings, after some dinner, I spent my time in our small room studying while my parents went to bed. The blackout presented some problems. It was prohibited for any light to be visible from outside the window, and there was also a restriction on the use of electricity. Studying by a kerosene lamp was an unsatisfactory solution to this problem, and I soon felt eye irritation and was uncomfortable in the restricted space. My parents also were disturbed by my activity while they wanted to sleep. My father found a way out. Close to where we lived, there was the office of the local German language newspaper — the *Shanghai Jewish Chronicle* — which had special permission to use electricity during the night, and Father got the consent of the editor for me to study there since there was a lot of unused space during the overnight hours. That arrangement worked really-ly well for me except that the proofreader often fell asleep at his desk, and I was tempted to take over rather than study. How I had the energy to help out at these times, I do not know. I was young, of course, and I also saw it as a challenge to learn how to proofread. At the same time, I was able to read the meager news they were allowed to print.

My pass expired at 8:00 p.m. and I was always anxious to arrive in the district on time. This presented a problem since I was entirely dependent on the public transportation system, whose performance was often spotty. One rainy winter evening while on my way home by tram, I realized to my horror that it was getting late and I would not be able to pass the border on time. I knew that there were Russian policemen working for the Japanese checking the passes as people descended from the tram at the last stop, and I could not expect any mercy from any of them. I did not know what the consequences would be if I arrived five to ten minutes late, and I was frightened. Many thoughts flashed through my mind. Would I be arrested and jailed? Would they give me a beating? The suspense was building and anxiety took possession of my whole being.

In fact, the policeman did check my pass, noted that I was late and took away my precious pass, the key to freedom beyond the district boundaries.

That night I did not sleep much since I was afraid of what would happen to me. I had seen a man, a refugee, who evidently had offended one of these Russian policemen being shoved through the entrance of the police station, and he was obviously terrified. I knew something of what lay beyond in the jail. I had heard from Father that several refugees, who had not complied with the requirement to relocate into the district, had been jailed there, and after they were released they all had come down with a disease called typhus, which had been propagated by fleas that infested the jail. These sick men were hospitalized in the district and were then transferred to a bigger hospital run by the Russian Jewish community, but most of them died shortly afterwards. I believe that there was no known cure for typhus at the time.

The possibility of being jailed terrified me. I was threatened to the core by the realization that I was powerless and completely at the mercy of the capricious decisions of the authorities who had unlimited power over my destiny and, indeed, over my life. I had had that same feeling of defenselessness in Vienna as a youngster after the Nazi-German takeover. I could not find peace in myself and spent the next two days in a state of near hysteria. At times, I was reduced to tears and remember overhearing Mother talk about this to another woman.

"I suffer seeing Otto being so tense and frightened, and at times crying. I find it terrible to see a young man at his age being in such a state and not being able to withhold tears."

She tried to comfort me, but I was not to be consoled. The image of my being dragged off to jail invaded my mind most of the time. I tried to read, but my concentration was only fleeting, and the dreaded image kept reappearing. Father kept his usual silence and stayed at some distance from me, although this was not easy in our confined quarters.

After two days, somebody told Father that my name was on the board at the police station. I went to Ghoya's office the next day and could barely control the trembling that shook my whole body as I got in line. My fate was about to be revealed. When my turn came to enter and to approach the official's desk, I was a nervous wreck. Ghoya held up my pass and mumbled:

"St. John's University is small university."

With these words, he handed me my pass. I clutched it and left the office. My body relaxed with the relief that came from the realization that I was free to go. Later, back at our room, I examined the pass and determined that I could still be outside the district during the same hours as before, but my privilege to visit one part of the city, called the "French Concession" had been revoked.

After some reflection, I decided that I would continue going to the homes of students I tutored who lived in that excluded area, but I would not tell anyone about it. While moving about there, I took off my badge to avoid attracting attention, reasoning that I would probably go unnoticed and unchallenged. During the months of my wandering about the French Concession legally, I had never experienced or observed any inspection. Looking back, I marvel at my courage to break the rules in spite of the danger I had sensed and the fear I had felt after my pass was confiscated. Probably, I was determined to keep for myself some limited measure of freedom.

In the course of the ensuing years, I returned late to the district several times. However, I had learned to avoid being caught. I got off the streetcar before arriving at the last stop and then made my way along side streets that were less closely monitored by refugee *bao jia* (guards) who were rarely supervised. The risk of getting caught and reported on this route was significantly reduced. The fact is that it worked for me. I felt good about rebelling, and getting away with it, against the otherwise overwhelming powers ranged against me.

Chapter 8

Liberation

"The Americans have dropped an atomic bomb on Japan! This is the story that is making the rounds. Can it be true? Can it be a "real atomic bomb?"

One of a group of students directed the question to the chemistry instructor, Mr. Shen, who was walking along with a group of us on our way home from the campus of St. John's University across the adjacent Jessfield Park (*Zhongshan Gongyuan*). It was August 8th 1945. I also had heard this rumor from several people and it had stimulated a great deal of excited speculation among fellow students, with my parents and in the homes of students I tutored.

What was true? What did it mean for us all living in this Japanese-occupied city, which had experienced increasingly heavy aerial bombardment by U.S. planes?

"Probably not," Mr. Shen replied, "I assume that it was a particularly powerful bomb and they called it an atomic bomb, just to make the event newsworthy. The construction of a 'real atomic bomb' must be a complex project on a large scale. Could such an undertaking be kept secret? No hint or threat of using such a weapon has reached the public media. Of course, we must remember that the Japanese authorities have kept a tight control over our media access here".

All of us students, having reached an intermediate level of scientific education, had only the vaguest idea of what a "real atomic bomb" might be.

"A second atomic bomb has been dropped on Japan," announced another fellow- student, Lu, to a group of us working in a laboratory two days later. It was now August 10th. "Thousands of people were killed by a single bomb," he continued.

I never knew where these news reports originated, nor how they reached the general public. It is my guess that increasing numbers of residents dared to transgress on the rules imposed by the Japanese, and listened to shortwave broadcasts of the BBC.

Some of us went to the library to look up the subject of uranium fission in journals dating from around 1940. We were motivated by the announcement of a second atomic bomb but were aware that we were limited to wild speculation, based on the outdated information we could access. Faculty members were of no help — they were as puzzled as we were. A group of students had assembled outside the library building and discussed what they had found in the old journals. Suggestions of what a "real atomic bomb" might be like were offered, discussed and discarded in quick succession. We were like a pack of wolves trying to find a path out of a dark forest. But we arrived at a consensus, that a "real atomic bomb" — a super-powerful weapon — had probably appeared on the world scene and that two such bombs had been dropped on Japan by American planes. We also concluded that, in all probability, an atomic bomb was capable of devastating an entire city, whatever its exact nature might be.

When walking home from the tram stop in the district that evening, I overheard snatches of excited conversation exchanged by residents of the Designated Area.

"The Americans have dropped atomic bombs on Japan."

"They have demanded the surrender of the Japanese army."

"The Japanese officials have left the police station, and refugees have occupied it!"

When I arrived home, I encountered residents of the house also in a state of excitement, confusion and uncertainty.

"What does it all mean?" many asked.

"Is this the end of the war?"

"Are we now free from the restrictions of the district?"

"Can we go and come as we wish?"

Nobody had the answers to these all-important questions.

"Yankee Doodle came to town, riding on his pony...." The strains reached my ears, emanating two days later from a radio in a room in the house as I was leaving for the university in the morning. **This was the signal for me that the war was** <u>really</u> **over!** Somebody at a local radio station must have found an old record that had escaped discovery.

That evening, on arriving home, I received additional confirmation from my father.

"The Japanese policemen returned to the station yesterday but they left again today and they told the crowd of refugees milling about that they were not coming back."

"If these latest attacks, using what they call "atomic bombs," force the Japanese to surrender and the war is over, it would be just in time — before we were all blown to smithereens by the American bombardments here in Shanghai," Father further commented, expressing the fears that many of us had felt for the past several months.

"There are Americans on campus," a fellow student said in my presence to a small group having lunch in the restaurant two days later (it was now August 14th). "I just saw them playing ball on the lawn," he added.

I could not contain myself and ran out to look. I saw about four or five men in T-shirts passing what seemed to be a softball among them. Overcoming my inhibitions, I went over to the group and addressed them:

"Hi there! I was told that you are Americans. Is that true?"

"You bet!" one of them responded.

"Where did you come from?" I inquired.

"From Pudong," was the reply.

I was stunned. The American said this as if it were the most natural thing in the world. Pudong (meaning east of the river) is just across the Huang-pu River from Shanghai! Just a few days before, all this territory had been occupied and controlled by the Japanese military! The Americans returned to their ball playing, and I took this as a signal that they discouraged further questioning. However, their presence and the exchange I had with them, however limited it was, surely constituted the final confirmation that the war was indeed over for us.

As all the world knows, the atomic bombs were dropped on Hiroshima and Nagasaki on August 6th and 9th, respectively, and on August 6th, President Truman informed the public in a press release of the first atomic bombing, followed by an address to the nation on August 9th. On August 15th, Emperor Hirohito of Japan made a widely publicized speech declaring that the Americans had used "a new and most cruel bomb, the power of which to do damage is indeed incalculable."

Emperor Hirohito went on to announce: "We have ordered our government to communicate to the Governments of the United States, Great Britain, China and the Soviet Union that our Empire accepts the provisions of their Joint Declaration."

The reference was to the so-called "Potsdam Declaration" that demanded the unconditional surrender of Japan. This Declaration was proclaimed following the first nuclear detonation test — dubbed the "Trinity Test" — which had been carried out successfully in the New Mexico desert on July 16th 1945, but no reference to this event was released to the public at the time.

Awareness of the implications of the end of the war took some time to sink in. However, the Jewish refugees who had been limited in their freedom of movement for over two years were eager to taste the immediate benefits. Anyone who had enough money to take a trip into town by public transportation took advantage of the newfound opportunity. The Russian policemen who used to hang around at the tram stop checking passes were gone. Revolutionary changes for the entire community were just around the corner. For the time being, there was the excitement of the liberation, and everyone was in a festive mood and celebrated to the best of their abilities.

"Meet me tonight at 8 at the corner near your house. My father has offered to give me money to celebrate!"

This was Maida speaking. She attended St. John's University, and I had often interacted with her — in fact I had attempted to court her without success. She lived somewhere outside the district but close by, and we had often walked large distances together on our way from the university although she was prosperous enough to own a bicycle. She was from Yugoslavia, I believe. I did not quite know what to make of her proposal, but I accepted without hesitation.

Sure enough, she was there at the appointed hour and handed me a wad of banknotes.

"My father said that this money will lose its value anyway, now that there will be a change of administration. Let's go and spend it."

We soon found a bar filled with people who laughed, sang and drank. We sat down with people whom I did not know but the mood was such that this was of no significance. A warm feeling of community had taken hold and everybody was open to embracing strangers as cocelebrants. I felt powerful with the bundle of Maida's money in my pocket and paid for many rounds of drinks and snacks. I made many new friends that night. Needless to say, I had not had any spare cash for a long time; actually never before had I been in this position of being able to throw money around, and I enjoyed the feeling of power that came with it. After all, it was not my money. I adjusted well to my newfound riches, however temporary they were, and was quite willing to faithfully obey the instructions Maida had given me to spend the money. Occasionally I overheard one of our fellow revelers whisper to a neighbor:

"Where did he get all this money from? Must be that the girl gave it to him."

I was not in a mood to worry about such comments and did not care what they thought of the situation or even what they thought of me. I floated well above the earth. We all soon were in a semi drunk blissful stupor and toasted freedom, liberation, the Americans and congratulated each other on our survival. I was swimming in a sea of happiness pervaded by glowing lights. And whenever the fog lifted, I went right back, drank some more and again immersed myself in a state where care and pain did not exist.

Maida and I finally left in the early hours of the morning as the crowds had thinned, and I was still high on the now fuzzy awareness that we had lived through an unforgettable and earth-shaking event that would change the course of our lives. I also experienced a surge of sexual desire, but Maida gently but firmly refused to cooperate. We parted after I returned to her the much diminished stash of her father's money. I have always looked back on this experience with satisfaction. I believe that it was proper and even ordained for this celebration to happen. I deserved it! Thank you, Maida, wherever you are.

Soon the Nationalist army of Chiang-Kai-Shek moved in. I saw columns of soldiers in bedraggled uniforms and straw sandals headed by well-uniformed officers move through the streets. Their rifles seemed to be all right — probably of United States manufacture. At least one of the columns was followed by a group of soldiers carrying bundles suspended from poles as was common in China. I remember being shocked at the sight. One day I came across a large crowd in the neighborhood of a Chinese theater. On inquiry, I was told that a group of Chinese soldiers had forced their way into the theater refusing to pay for their tickets, and they had fired off guns as Chinese MPs arrived. Sure enough, I soon saw Chinese MPs load a group of the offenders onto a truck and take them away. To me this was indicative of the quality of the "victorious Nationalist Chinese army." No wonder they did not prevail against the Communists! In fairness, I must add that I also eventually witnessed drunk American sailors being picked up by MPs, but they obviously had respect for the military law enforcers.

Shanghai was soon transformed. The city filled up with United States service personnel, mostly army and navy, who were funneled out through the port from the entire CBI (China-Burma-India) theater of war on their way home. PXs (Retail Stores for American Servicemen) and USOs (Social Activity Centers for American Servicemen) were opened, United States army trucks filled the streets, and everybody who could walk could get trained, get a job, and get paid well in United States greenbacks. Women of all ages, it seemed, were in great demand, and we, residents, had no chance to get dates for a long time. The competition was too fierce.

I did not join the rush to employment by the Americans. I continued my studies and my tutoring of high school students. However, my outlook toward the future underwent a drastic change.

"I have been thinking of continuing my studies in the United States after graduation here," I told my parents one day in the fall of 1945. "What do you think? And what do you plan to do, now that the war is over and the Americans have come and liberated us?"

The world had opened up, and I could suddenly think and dream of a future which had been outside the realm of possibility for so long. I did really think of Americans as the redeemers. They had freed the world of the scourge of fascism and the danger of Japanese domination. The Americans were the ultimate heroes! They even supplied the refugees with cartons of food distributed by UNRRA (United Nations Relief and Rehabilitation Administration).

"We will try to join Herta in Kenya," was Father's reply. "I had thought that you would come with us.

At least Herta has mentioned that possibility in her letters. You might think about it and decide where you stand. I don't see how you can go off all by yourself to the United States without money. It is all right to dream, but actually realizing the dream is another matter. How would you get a visa, and how would you get there?"

I had to admit that there were many hurdles to overcome, and I did not have good answers at the time. However, I refused to give up and continued to plan and plot. I had survived the war years under Japanese occupation and American bombardment. I also had begun to learn what suffering and danger to my life I had escaped by being taken away from Vienna, primarily thanks to the determination of my father combined with the money my grandfather had accumulated and left to my grandmother. The fates had conspired to let me survive against odds beyond what I could conceive. I accepted the obligation to honor this miracle and to do my part to lead a full and productive life. I was not yet ready, but, in time, I was determined to take on the world!

Chapter 9

Leaving Shanghai

After the end of the war, I moved to the St. John's University campus and lived there with another Jewish refugee student in a dormitory building. Our room was stark and devoid of comfort or warmth. Four whitewashed walls and the minimum of furniture — two iron bedsteads, two chairs, a small table and a recess in the wall equipped with a wooden rod to hang clothes. The great benefits of living there were that it saved some money and two whole hours a day, which I had spent on public transportation getting to and from school.

"Here is a piece of news that will interest you!" my father exclaimed when I came home for a visit one weekend in late 1946.

Otto Schnepp

"I have a patient, an older American GI called Fred, who is grateful for the help I've given him. He suffered from a pernicious skin disease for years and had not been able to get rid of it. He had consulted many specialists in the course of the years, and I succeeded in curing him. He told me the other day that he is indeed grateful and wants to do something for me. I said that there is nothing I needed but that it would be great if he could help you get to America to do graduate work. He suggested that you write to him after he returns to the United States. He is scheduled to leave, or to `ship out,' as he put it, next week."

"Wow," I responded, "that sounds really great! Thank you so much for doing this! If he will help me, that may really make a difference."

"Just don't pin too much hope on this offer," Father warned. "People often offer help and then don't come through in the end."

I followed up and wrote to Fred. He responded graciously and assured me that he was serious about this offer. He even offered to make an effort to connect me with his own Alma Mater. I was to graduate in June 1947 and was gearing up to apply to various universities, including UC Berkeley, where I was eventually accepted but without their recognizing my degree from St. John's. Fred offered to send me a monthly stipend and agreed to the modest sum I suggested — I believe it was $75.

"Mr. Jordan wants you to make an appointment to see him," Peter said as he came for his scheduled lesson. "I assume that he wants to ask for your opinion of me."

I had been tutoring Peter for the past three months to prepare him for an examination in lieu of a high school diploma. He had ambitions to apply to an American university. Peter was working for Charles Jordan, the director of the Shanghai office of the Jewish Joint Distribution Committee. In this capacity he was responsible for the movement of thousands of refugees to the United States and other destinations. The quota system in force at the time allowed for the immigration of people who had been born in Germany.

"What do you think of Peter?" Mr. Jordan asked, coming straight to the point. "I want to help him, but I want your opinion of his chances for success in a college environment. Please give me your assessment of his intellectual capability."

I remember feeling challenged by this powerful man and did my best. I had had time to prepare myself, and when I left the office, I had the sense that he was satisfied with my response and that I had made a favorable impression.

"Let me know if you need any help in the future," were Mr. Jordan's parting words. I could not think of any need for help at the moment, but little did I know how crucial a role Mr. Jordan was to play in my life.

My parents left Shanghai in April 1947 and went to join my sister Herta who lived in Nairobi, the capital city of Kenya, at the time a British Crown Colony in East Africa. Herta had first assumed that I would join my parents and come with them. However, I made the choice of staying in Shanghai to complete my undergraduate degree. I planned to try to get to the United States for graduate studies after graduation. Soon after my parents' departure, the awareness of my being all alone in the world flooded my consciousness. This was a world that predated readily available and reliable international telephone service, and postal service took weeks by ship.

There were many uncertainties in my future. I had been admitted to UC Berkeley although it was

conditional on my fulfilling undergraduate requirements for another bachelor's degree. I also had the
promise from my father's former patient, Fred, to
send me monthly checks, and I had saved up $500
to get me started. But could I get a visa to the United
States? And did I have the intellectual capacity to
succeed at an American university? These were un-
knowns that weighed on my mind.

In June 1947, I graduated from St. John's and that
day, after the ceremony, there were many celebra-
tions on campus. One building in particular was all
lit up, and people went in and out talking excitedly
and laughing — graduates, their families and
friends. I sat alone under a large camphor tree near
the entrance of that busy building that evening. I
allowed the feelings of lonliness and isolation to
flood over me for an hour or so. Then I picked myself up and walked to my dormitory room and read
myself to sleep.

During the summer and fall of 1947, I directed
my thoughts and energies to achieving my goal of
getting a U.S. visa to allow me to continue my studies at UC Berkeley. Since my country of birth was
Austria, I could not obtain an Immigration Visa —
the quota was minimal, and it would have taken

years for me to qualify. The other alternative was a Student Visa. I went to the United States Consulate and showed the letter I had from my sponsor, Fred, promising a monthly stipend. I also produced American Express travelers' checks for $500, which represented the sum total of my savings.

"This will get you nowhere. This letter is no guarantee; it has no legal standing," the official told me with a wave of his hand accompanying his response. "In order to get a student visa you need to prove that you have $2,000."

I had been dismissed and needed to explore possibilities of raising the required money guarantee. I had acquired my American Express checks with the help of an old friend who worked at a hotel where many Americans stayed. He bought the checks with local currency, and the American Express office issued checks in my name in exchange for the original ones. This was a completely legal procedure.

"I want to make you a proposition," Mr. Weiss, the father of my girlfriend, said to me a few days after my visit to the Consulate. "I will provide you with local currency equivalent to $500 if you can buy United States dollars and deliver this money to a trusted friend of mine in Oakland."

I was delighted. This proposal was well-timed, and now I could show that I had $1,000 to my name. I also felt honored by the fact that Mr. Weiss was willing to trust me to fulfill my end of the bargain. After all, he had no control over my actions after I left Shanghai.

My next move was to make an appointment with Mr. Jordan. Now I needed help. When I explained my problem and showed him the letter from Fred and the checks, he was upbeat and agreed to help.

"I will call the Consulate," Mr. Jordan said.

"He has a bona fide letter guaranteeing monthly support," he told the Consul with whom he obviously had a good working relationship.

It was to no avail. The Consul insisted that I needed to prove that I had $2,000 as required by the regulations. I left Mr. Jordan's office feeling discouraged and seeing my chances for going to the United States slip away.

As I left the office, I saw Mr. Silberberg in the waiting room. I knew him from my activities in the labor Zionist youth organization, Habonim; he was one of the Senior sponsors of the local chapter. He had expressed his appreciation for my plans to go to Israel after completion of my education. I sat down next to him and poured out my heart to him. To my surprise, he did not just sympathize, but offered his help.

"I would be traveling on the same ship with you," Mr. Silberberg said. "Mr. Jordan will issue me a letter guaranteeing the payment of a sum of money through a bank in San Francisco.

Perhaps he would be willing to issue a letter to you for the $1,000 you need. Then, when we arrive in San Francisco, you can cash the money and give it to me."

My spirits picked up again, and we went in together to Mr. Jordan's office on the strength of Mr. Silberberg's appointment, and we explained the suggested offer of help.

"Can you help Otto?" Mr. Silberberg concluded.

Mr. Jordan's face became pensive, and his forehead was furrowed. I was tense and held my breath. My heart beat like a jungle drum. I thought the other two men must have been able to hear it pound away. Finally, after what seemed an eternity to me, he spoke.

"Here is what I will do. I will help, and I will issue this letter you ask for."

I breathed again. Then, Mr. Jordan turned to me and faced me squarely.

"If you ever tell on me, I will find you, and I will break your neck! Good luck."

With these friendly words, softened by a smile, we parted.

So armed with a modest amount of money of my own, borrowed money and the letter of support from the United Jewish Appeal, I finally obtained my visa. I set out on my adventure of getting myself an education at Berkeley armed, as well, with the promise of support from my American benefactor.

However, I was burdened by a great deal of insecurity. I still had to earn admission to graduate school and faced financial uncertainty. Most importantly, I did not know how I would measure up to the intellectual challenges of my new environment.

One day in January 1948, I set sail from Shanghai, my city of refuge from the Holocaust, which had taken the lives of family members and friends. I was bound for Berkeley where I was to fend for myself and hoped to succeed in getting an advanced education that was to prepare me for my future in the newly established state of Israel.

Otto Schnepp

Many years later, I heard that Mr. Jordan had been active in Europe, including Eastern Europe, on behalf of Jewish communities during the 1960s, still in the employ of the United Jewish Appeal. It was reported that he had visited Prague with his wife in August 1967. He left the hotel one evening and never returned.

His bloated body was found four days later by a fisherman in the Vltava (Moldau) River which flows through Prague. To the best of my knowledge, the facts surrounding Jordan's death have never been clarified, even after the demise of the Soviet Empire allowed access to a wealth of secret documents. An article describing the known facts concerning his disappearance and death was published in the International Herald Tribune of February 29, 2000, page 2, on the occasion of a meeting of Jewish leaders in Prague to memorialize Charles Jordan and his numerous contributions to Jewish communities throughout Communist Eastern Europe.

I was shocked by this news and mourned the loss of a man who had worked hard to better the lives of others, including my own. I owed him a deep debt of gratitude for his unselfish support, and for the risk he took in helping me. I have come to understand that Jordan was a man who accepted that risk-taking was intrinsic to his professional life. Unfortunately, it seems that he took one risk too many.

Chapter 10

From Shanghai to San Francisco

In January 1948, I embarked in Shanghai on a converted WWII troop transport ship named *General Meigs*, to begin the great adventure of my graduate studies at the University of California, Berkeley. After surviving WWII and a series of sometimes seemingly desperate attempts and rejections, I finally achieved my aim and obtained a student visa from the U.S. Consulate in Shanghai. This had been a challenging process, and I had been close to giving up several times. It had taken the intervention of several personages who had come to my aid and whom, it seemed, some fairy spirit had recruited to support me in my struggle. The central hurdle was the requirement to prove that I had $2,000 at my disposal, and I have described the circuitous route by which I finally succeeded in achieving this goal.

Three friends had appeared to wave me farewell — my girlfriend Eva and two young students of Russian Jewish parentage, Danya and Renya (Dan and René) who had come to Shanghai from Tianjin to study engineering at the French university, L'Université Aurore. I remember them standing on the pier, and I was on the deck of the ship. We waved to each other, having no idea if we would ever see each other again. I did see Eva again many years later, but only eventually connected with Renya by email. This was yet another parting experience, with mixed emotions: sadness at leaving a place where I had spent nine difficult but formative years, and from the many connections I had formed there. There also was the excitement mixed with anxiety as I looked forward to my next and, what turned out to be, significant life experience.

So here I was, with a small part of the total sum of $2,000 I needed in order to prove to the consul that what I had at my disposal was really mine, and facing the future with much uncertainty. I anticipated residing and studying in the U.S. with a number of restrictions, particularly concerning my ability to earn money. A holder of a student visa was required to be registered at an institution of higher learning and to be in good standing at all times and, moreover, any work had to be such as could be considered related to the visa holder's educational goals. This visa contrasted sharply with an immigration visa, which gave the holder full freedom of residency including unlimited permission to work and a pathway to citizenship after five years. At the time, the issuance of immigration visas was governed by the quota system based on the country of birth, and the Austrian quota was very small and prevented me from obtaining one of those visas. On the other hand, all refugees in Shanghai who had been born in Germany could obtain such a visa as long as an individual or an organization sponsored them — the latter was an innovation enacted after the end of WWII. The United Jewish Appeal of the United States supported the immigration of many thousands of Holocaust survivors.

As a young man of 22, I was alone in the wide world. My parents had left for East Africa to join my sister, and the means of communication in 1948 were nothing like those we have at the present time. There was the mail, of course, but it took close to a month for a letter to cross the distance from Shanghai or Berkeley to Nairobi in Kenya. There was actually no way I could get financial support, if needed, both because neither my parents nor my sister had the resources, and because there also were serious restrictions in force on money transfers because of what was called at the time, the "sterling block." A collective name for coutries using the currency of pound sterling. However, it had been my decision not to join my parents since I had wanted to complete my B.S. studies at St. John's University and then to find my way to the United States for graduate studies.

As I set sail for California, I was uncertain and often anxious about my chances for academic success at U.C. Berkeley. Judging by grades, I had been no more than a passable student at St. John's University in Shanghai. True, I had been forced to spend a lot of time tutoring high school students who needed help adjusting to changes in curriculum as circumstances forced them to transfer schools during the war and immediately after its conclusion in 1945. Later, I had had a part-time job teaching math and physics at the Shanghai Jewish School. This was how I supported myself. Further, I did not have any clear plan for long-term financial support. The money I had would barely be enough to get through a year or so. But I was young and knew that I had a passion for science and mathematics. I also had the promise of a grateful former patient of my father's to send me a small monthly stipend. Armed with these strengths, I set out to conquer the world or, at least, more realistically, to find a niche for myself in it. I did have an escape plan in case I failed to make it in graduate school: I would make my way to Israel, which was on the verge of being established in May 1948. I had, in fact, decided to end up there after completing a graduate degree, assuming I accomplished that goal.

The passengers on the ship were, to the best of my knowledge, all Jewish refugees who had survived the war in Shanghai, and with few exceptions, were traveling to the United States on immigration visas issued on the German quota and sponsored by the United Jewish Appeal. They were all stimulated by their hopes for their new lives, and conversations mostly centered on their expectations, although some of them allowed their anxieties to show as well. I mostly interacted with young people who, like myself, had benefited from a basic school education in English, and many had experienced contacts managed to transform Japan from an Empire ruled by the military into a democracy.

All along the route taken by the bus, there was nothing but utter devastation following the heavy bombardment by the U.S. Air Force that had crippled Japanese industry and caused terrible loss of life in Tokyo and its surroundings. The heavy bombers were four-engine planes (B-29s) flying from the base at Kunming in Yun'nan province located in southwest China, beyond the reach of the Japanese army that had invaded China beginning in 1937. During the latter part of the war, we had become well-acquainted with these planes that frequently attacked targets in the Shanghai area. We were told that the stretch between Yokohama and Tokyo had been a heavily industrialized zone. The destruction was so complete that it seemed no building had been left standing, and it was improbable that anyone could have survived.

I have only vague memories of Tokyo from this visit. I do recall that it appeared to be a war-ravaged and dead city with much visible destruction and not much sign of activity. It offered a drab scene with barely a few active construction sites providing some hints of rebuilding and offering a glimmer of hope for the future. There was the sparsest of traffic. It is hard to imagine that this city, so alive and bustling during subsequent visits over the past thirty years beginning in 1969, could have been the same place.

The next port of call was Honolulu. Hawaii and Honolulu stood in stark contrast to my Tokyo experience. I found the pleasant, sunny weather and the eye-pleasing countryside, with colorful flowing hills, delightful. The local Jewish community had prepared a welcome program, including the mandatory Hula dance entertainment and distribution of leis to the visitors. A group of three or four young men close to my age took me for a tour of the city, and I was impressed with the beauty of the verdant and lush landscape and the obvious opulence of the society. It was as if I had arrived on another planet. One of the stops was the Royal Hawaiian Hotel where I tasted pineapple juice from a freely flowing fountain in the foyer. As I found out on subsequent visits to Honolulu, these fountains have unfortunately disappeared. However, I have had my recollection confirmed during a chance encounter much later with a Hawaiian resident of my generation who also remembered this miracle-like vision.

ROOTS LOST-ROOTS FOUND

A few days following our visit to Honolulu, it was announced that early the next morning we would enter San Francisco Bay through the storied Golden Gate on the way to the dock. I was up before dawn that morning, and so were many of my co-passengers. We did not want to miss anything of our arrival to mainland United States of America. It was a great moment when the Golden Gate Bridge emerged from the fog in front of the ship's bow — an unforgettable experience. For most of us, it was the fulfillment of a long-held dream. We were about to arrive in the promised land from which our saviors had come, liberated us from the Japanese occupation and had opened up the path to rebuilding our lives, offering us hope for a bright future.

I retain a clear memory of my first glimpses of the city. The morning was just dawning as we passed under the lofty towers of the bridge and entered the Bay. The city was mysteriously shrouded in the early morning mist through which I could discern the city lights revealing the straight lines of streets descending to the bay. The ship then tied up at one of the piers at the Embarcadero.

Immigration officers came aboard to process the new arrivals, and then we were free to disembark. I had some financial obligation to settle, escorted by my Labor-Zionist friend who had played a central part in the process of my being issued a visa. I spent the first night at a small hotel on Mason Street, after walking the neighboring streets to get oriented. I contacted a friend from Shanghai who lived in Berkeley who had promised to help me on arrival.

The next morning before being picked up to cross the Bay, I had breakfast in a cafeteria where I observed the proceedings before venturing to get in line. I spoke English very well, of course, and certainly did not expect to have any difficulty in this department. When my turn came, I asked for fried eggs, and the cook shot back: "up or over?" and I was stumped. I did understand, however, that I owed a quick answer and replied "up," just because it was the first choice offered. I had never before encountered fried eggs served "over" or "over easy." So much for my arrogant assumption that I had full command of the English language!

My major anxiety concerned my finding the means — regarding both financial and immigration status — to stay in the United States for an extended period to complete an advanced degree. I recall that I had real feelings of envy for the security,that I at least imagined the local residents felt in having a home, no matter how modest. I was alone and adrift in the wide world without anchor or security and without any recourse to family advice or backing. I was, of course, fully responsible for creating this situation by having cut myself loose from all the usual moorings that I had judged unsuitable to my goals.

Another major area of insecurity concerned my future as a student. I simply did not know if I would succeed or perhaps fail miserably in the strange,and very different environment. And if I should fail - what then? Where could I go? Fortunately, the State of Israel was in the process of taking shape — it was emerging from a vortex of struggle and warfare — and nobody knew at the time what the outcome would be. I carried an Austrian passport but had no intention of settling there; I had strong feelings of enmity approaching hatred for the Austrian people who had so rejected me and mine and had been active participants in our expulsion and banishment under threat of violence. At the time we did not know to what extent the Germans and Austrians were willing to go. My close family — parents and sister — were far away and I had chosen a path for

Chapter 11

Berkeley

With the help of my Shanghai friend in Berkeley, who had promised to help me upon my arrival, I moved into a hotel in Berkeley for a few days while investigating and considering my options. I next moved into an old-style, wooden rooming house where students and other young people lived. For meals, I chose to join a students' co-op as a boarder, which was inexpensive but required me to work three hours a week waiting tables or dishwashing. I soon became adept at the required skills.

I got in touch with some Shanghai youths whom I knew, hoping to get guidance from them in the ways of the university. However, I soon found out that their experiences were not relevant to my plans since they were not into science studies. They did, however, describe some disturbing experiences relating to midterms and examinations, claiming that often questions asked had not been covered in the material presented or assigned. These threatening tales added to the store of anxieties that were already besetting me, but eventually turned out to be exaggerated. These were typical of the stories people tell to impress or intimidate a newcomer.

I registered successfully for my first semester at UC-Berkeley and was reasonably successful, academically. I did, however, get one grade of C in an Inorganic Chemistry course (required for my BA degree), but I managed to get the highest score in another course in which only graduate students and seniors participated. Fortunately this course had a great deal of stature in this department and I derived some healthy recognition from this success.

After the spring semester and two summer sessions I received my degree and was accepted to graduate school, aiming at a Ph.D. degree. In addition, I received a teaching assistant's position with attached benefits that included an assured modest income in excess of my budget up to this point, and a considerable reduction of my fees as a California resident. My monthly salary, I recall, was $120 with about $10 being deducted for taxes. I was now set for my studies and had won my place in the sun, or so it seemed to me. At least I was now launched on a trajectory to be tested if I was of intellectual caliber for a Ph.D. from Berkeley. As a result I was now in a position to proudly announce to my American bene-factor that I no longer required his financial support and could now stand on my own two feet.

As time went on, I became increasingly secure as my studies progressed successfully and I proved myself equal to the best among the graduate stu-dents. I soon found a home in a research group with a direction that thoroughly satisfied my interests in physical chemistry, and I began pursuing research projects on the border between the two disciplines (physics and chemistry). I also had some gratifying experiences teaching laboratory courses and found satisfaction from good relations with the under-graduates in my sections. I was enormously pleased and proud when one section (about 20-25 students) presented me with a pen at the end of a semester in appreciation of my service to them.

Otto Schnepp

This was a period of intensive intellectual growth in an exciting and motivating environment, the likes of which I had never known. I learned what it was like to be in touch with the frontiers of science and to be exposed to leaders in various fields from around the country and the world, in addition to the distinguished faculty at Berkeley. I audited courses given by visiting scientists who were giants in their fields including Robert Oppenheimer, who had been the director of the atomic bomb project code-named the Manhattan Project during WWII, and Enrico Fermi, who had directed the first chain reaction involving nuclear fission at the University of Chicago. I took courses taught by illustrious local faculty including future Nobel laureates Francis Giauque, who had experimentally confirmed the Third Law of Thermodynamics, Glenn T. Seaborg, the creator of the trans-uranian elements (including plutonium) and Emilio Segrè, who had discovered the first man-made element, technetium, and the fissionable isotope of plutonium. Segrè later co-discovered the first anti-particle, the anti-proton, which has the same mass as the proton but carries a negative charge, whereas the proton carries a positive charge. It was this latter work which earned Segrè and his coworker, Carlo Perrier, the Nobel Prize. Together with many more near-equally famous scientists, there were at the University of California, Berkeley, quite a dizzying array of science greats whose mere presence was inspiring and highly motivating for young scholars like myself.

During this period I experienced my first sexual love affair with a student called Anne. This experience was certainly formative and enriching, although the relationship was limited by the young woman's psychological wounds. In later years, I hypothesized that my attraction to neurotic women may have been related to my mother's life-long tendency to depression. My relationship with Anne lasted from mid-1948 until early 1950 when I decided to give it up because of the hurt I suffered periodically that eventually outweighed the benefits, which were considerable. Anne was a highly intelligent and passionate young woman, and we had a lot of good times. We traveled to Los Angeles together (my very first visit) to attend the Rose Bowl game on 1 January 1949 in which UC Berkeley was defeated by Northwestern University.

Chapter 12

From Berkeley
to Israel

In preparation for the move to Israel after completing my post-doctoral year, I had responded to an advertisement from the Technion, originally an engineering college in the port city of Haifa that was renamed the Israel Institute of Technology. The administration had made the decision to open science departments that would offer both undergraduate and graduate degrees and to assume the responsibility for teaching basic sciences to the engineering students. Fortunately, a professor of Applied Mathematics at UC Berkeley had recently spent a semester at the Technion and he supported my application after checking out my references at Berkeley. In time, I received an offer of a junior position designated "Lecturer" in the Physical Chemistry section of the newly established Chemistry Department to begin in October 1952. I happily accepted this offer, which included payment of moving expenses for my wife Miriam and me. [See Chapter 19 for more about Miriam and the other women in my life.] They also included an apartment in a group of newly-erected Swedish prefabricated houses in Ahuza, a neighborhood on Mt. Carmel in Haifa.

The time had arrived for preparations in earnest for our journey to Haifa. Mindful of my future teaching obligations in the Hebrew language, I sought out the help of an Israeli student to give me lessons during my last year in Berkeley. Miriam completed her B.A. degree in June and found a secretarial job for the summer. This additional income allowed us to purchase some furniture and appliances — a new refrigerator and an old-fashioned-type washing machine with a wringer mounted on top.

Next we faced the task of planning for transporting these newly acquired possessions to faraway Israel. I felt an obligation to minimize the cost and explained my reasoning to Miriam:

"I feel an obligation to economize on the moving expenses and will try to crate the furniture and appliances and ship them without engaging a mover."

Miriam responded: "I don't know how you can do this, but if that is what you want to do, go ahead and try. I don't think the Technion will refuse to add the necessary expenses to the cost of moving us, as long as they are within reasonable limits."

I rented a garage in the neighborhood where I stored and modified used crates, collected from various stores. Next, the crates had to be transported to the port of Alameda where I had located a shipping company that would accept the cargo for transporting to Haifa. For this final step, I recruited the entire research group, including our research director, Donald. When I gathered the group and gave them a tour of the crates, Donald was doubtful.

"We will need a crane to load all this onto the rented truck," Don said. "We can't lift these large crates."

But another doctoral student, John, spoke up: "I think we can do it if all five of us are willing to pitch in. I have some experience with loading. These crates are not all that heavy."

We agreed to assemble the next day, John rented the truck and we made our attempt to load the cargo onto the truck and to deliver it to the port. And we managed it with John driving. It turned out that there was some paperwork to be dealt with and finally the crates were on the loading dock of the shipping company. The final step was the inspection and acceptance by a shipping clerk. This turned out to be a friendly fellow who sympathized with my inexperience and was helpful. He then looked at the destination address painted on the crates and exclaimed;

"Israel — this is Jerusalem or something! Then you must be Jewish!"

I confirmed that indeed I was Jewish. The clerk's face then lit up in a broad grin and he exclaimed enthusiastically: "I am Irish!"

I did not understand the background of this reaction and my colleagues explained to me how Jewish and Irish immigrants had a history of cooperating in East Coast cities. Also at the time, Israel had recently been established after some years of resistance against the British rulers of Palestine and the Irish had their own history of struggle for independence from British rule.

ROOTS LOST-ROOTS FOUND

In the midst of all these preparations and hopes for the future, a letter arrived from my sister, Herta, from Nairobi, Kenya, with a troubling message. My mother, who had traveled to East Africa with my father from Shanghai in April 1947, had suffered from depression in later life. After my father's death in June 1952, Herta had taken her in to stay with her family. One morning, Herta found her in her room with bloodied wrists, evidently from a suicide attempt. Mother was transported to a hospital, and after some recovery period, was transferred to a rest home. Herta had married another refugee from Vienna who had come to Nairobi with his family. They had two daughters, at the time aged one and six. She wrote:

"You have to help us, we simply don't see any other solution than sending mother to Israel after your arrival there. The rest home is no permanent solution. There must be some arrangement you will be able to find there for Mother. I am terrified at the thought of my older daughter, Susan, finding her after another suicide attempt. Of course, we will help financially."

This letter arrived in Berkeley in July. Miriam was understandably upset at this turn of events.

"How will we manage there, in a strange country where we don't know our way around and now we will have to take care of your mother in addition? I am also frightened by the idea of living in a small apartment with somebody who may attempt or commit suicide any day!"

After a short and tense silence I responded:

"Look, there is no way I can refuse to take care of Mother after being at a distance for all these years. The best we can do under the circumstances is to postpone solving our problems until we come face to face with them and understand what tools we have at our disposal to deal with them. Let us deal with our plans for the trip meanwhile. I am confident that I will be able to get advice and help from people at the Technion."

I put up a good front, but in my heart I was not so sure. I was troubled, but held in all my anxiety and tensions. It was to take a long time until I learned to be in touch with my feelings and to share them with an intimate. It was a long and difficult path for me to climb back from my accumulated traumas to being fully human.

In early September 1952 we set out on our journey to Israel. Herta and her husband Willie planned to come to England to meet us on arrival in Southampton. I had last seen Herta in August 1938, just about 14 years before.

We crossed the continent by railway, with a stop in Chicago where we looked up old friends from Shanghai and then on to New York. We had booked passage from there to Southampton on the *Queen Elizabeth* of the Cunard Lines. This ship is often referred to as a luxury liner, but they also provided for the less than rich; we had a small cabin with bunk beds and a sink. This was September 1952 and transatlantic traffic by air had not yet become the primary mode of travel. We did not have a private bathroom and showers were not part of the dominant British culture, I inferred. We could order baths and these were prepared by crew members, a male for me and a female for Miriam. They would knock at our door and proclaim: "bath sir!" Or "bath ma'am!" We appreciated these ceremonial announcements with their sterling English accent as a pleasant and quaint touch. The water in the tub was salt water and a basin of fresh water was provided for a final rinse. The passage from New York to Southampton took about a week.

Otto Schnepp

As we left the ship, I easily recognized Herta in spite of the 14 years' separation. She was 16 years old when she left Vienna and she had not changed a whole lot. I ran up to her and gave her a big hug. Next I shook hands with Willie. He seemed friendly enough but hugging did not feel appropriate — perhaps it was the English influence.

"Herta, I recognized you immediately. But how did you recognize me, or did you?" I asked excitedly.

"I recognized you by your walk," Herta responded, "You always had a characteristic walk like our father's. When you walked with him, this was particularly apparent. The image has stuck in my mind. Come, let us collect your luggage and load it into the boot of our rented car. We will motor to London as quickly as we can."

The English terms were noticeable and set us apart. We spoke different languages after all! Miriam and I soon came to know that in England everyone immediately took us for Americans, no matter how hard we tried to imitate an English accent. While in the United States, I was often asked and am still sometimes asked if I am English. I was reminded of my interview for a job, shortly after graduating from high school in Shanghai, with Mr. Thomson of Thomson & Co., Chartered Accountants. Mr. Thomson asked me:

"Did you have much to do with Americans? You sound much like an American. Doesn't sound good to the ear of an Englishman, you know!"

This was the last of the British Empire speaking soon after Pearl Harbor and the occupation of the International Settlement of Shanghai by the Japanese army.

In London we met some relatives of Willie's and I also discovered that my uncle Gyuri Roth (Gyuri is an Hungarian diminutive and endearment for George) was listed in the telephone directory. I did know that he lived in the London area. I called and we had an exciting meeting and reunion. Herta and Willie showed us some of the famous sites. We then traveled to Paris — they by air I believe, and we by train and ferry — and we stayed in the same hotel, the Étoile, very close to the Champs Élysées, a very exciting area with the Arc de Triomph. We also visited the Place Pigalle, a notorious landmark known for striptease clubs, which aroused my curiosity.

I had made arrangements to visit a laboratory and met with a scientist with whom I had corresponded and discussed some of my work. This was a heady experience — a first outside the United States. I am afraid I bored Herta and Willie with my excited reports of this encounter. For me, it was stimulating to have some of my own research to talk about. We all avoided saying much about Mother and the plans to have her come to Israel. We were not ready to face all this and I, for one, preferred to stay with the high spirits of the reunion and the adventure of seeing and experiencing famous sights.

The four of us parted in Paris. They returned to Kenya and we continued to Israel, by way of Rome and Naples. We also saw some parts of ancient Rome and visited Pompeii on the way. These made memorable impressions on us on this first visit.

In Naples we boarded an Israeli ship sailing to Haifa. Traveling on a ship flying the Israeli flag with the Star of David and manned by an all-Jewish crew filled me with pride after all my Nazi experiences. These pleasurable feelings helped push the problems that lay in the future, however near, into the background.

As we came close to the coast, one Israeli fellow-passenger said to me with some pride showing in his voice:

"You know, we are now already in *Mare Nostrum*," (Latin for 'Our Sea'), an often-used term to designate territorial waters. This pronouncement has stuck in my mind. After more than 2,000 years we now had a land of our own, complete with a sea of our own. And I was going to have a tiny part in it. This was significant and, I believe, even contributed to my recovery from the trauma of feeling stateless and defenseless.

On arrival in the port of Haifa, we were all given numbers with the instruction to disembark as our numbers were called. Like well-disciplined Americans, we waited as we were told. But then we realized that the ship was already empty! Clearly others were not that disciplined. Dora, a representative of the Technion, met us. She helped us with the formalities, mainly by repeating the words *"Zeh beseder,"* meaning "it is O.K." Dora explained to me that this was the Hebrew password from the times of the underground resistance army *Hagana,* before the establishment of the State.

Dora took us to a simple hotel. At this time (October 1952), just barely two years after the armistice between Israel and its Arab neighbors ended the "War of Independence," most everything in Israel was termed *tsena,* meaning simplicity. So this was a *tsena* hotel equipped with *tsena* furniture and, I presume, a tsena staff.

We walked to the Technion, and found the Physical Chemistry section located in an addition to the campus, where I met the limited faculty, consisting of an older man, Dr. Garbatzki, who held the rank of Senior Lecturer and had received a doctorate from the University of Berlin before immigrating to Palestine. There were also two assistants, doctoral students who had been launched in research projects by a visiting professor from Howard University. He had returned to the United States, leaving them in Dr. Garbatzki's charge and in correspondence contact with the professor. It was, I concluded, a *tsena* faculty. There clearly was a lot of building-up work to be done.

A few days later, we were taken to an *ulpan* (a Hebrew language school for immigrants) in Nahariya, a town on the Mediterranean coast, north of Haifa, settled and at the time still populated by German Jewish immigrants. This was a boarding school, housed in a hotel, used previously for vacationers. The story went that there had been a dispute related to the armistice agreement concerning the fate of

Nahariya being located in the Jewish part (by then Israel) or Palestinian part, administered by the Kingdom of Jordan in accordance with the United Nations partition plan for Palestine. People said that no matter where Nahariya belonged, *es bleibt immer Deutsch* (it always remains being German).

We stayed at this *ulpan* for five months, just one month short of the full course. I was enrolled in the advanced class, and Miriam in the beginners' class. I took my Hebrew studies seriously, devoting nine hours a day, six days a week to them. We were then moved to our apartment in Haifa and I began teaching. I have referred to being "thrown to the students" although the experience was nothing like the encounters of the Christians with the lions during Roman times. Nevertheless, my early years of living in Israel and teaching in Hebrew were challenging.

The two assistants taught in the laboratory Physical Chemistry course for junior chemical engineering students, where I was first launched into teaching in Hebrew. The next semester I taught my first lecture course of Physical Chemistry for the first class of chemistry majors in their junior year, and I went on from there. I soon introduced a new course for seniors, and eventually added a graduate course after

Chapter 13

Adventures in the Israeli Army Reserves

"Hamdulillah!" I exclaimed in a state of shock, as I was handed my personal weapon and stared, in a state of disbelief, at the markings engraved on the lock of the rifle.

"Is this what I came to Israel for?"

I used the newly-learned Arabic exclamation, in wide use in Israeli slang, as the Nazi *Hoheitswappen* — an eagle bearing in its claws a wreath with the swastika at its center — stared up at me and clashed with my state of consciousness. Was this reality or was it a bad dream? I had come to Israel to finally feel that I was at home, where I was wanted and accepted. And here I was thrown back into memories of the horrors of Nazi Germany.

A fellow reservist noticed my state of consternation, and called out to me.

"Have you never seen a Czech rifle before?"

I was puzzled and also glad that somebody was willing to talk to me about my traumatic experience.

"What is a Czech rifle?" I inquired, hoping to be thrown a rope to help me pull myself out of my bewilderment.

"They were bought from the Soviets at the time of the War of Liberation in 1947/48. We desperately needed weapons to defend ourselves against the Arab armies that converged on us, but the West had imposed an arms embargo on the entire Middle East. The armies of the Arab states, of course, were armed. The USSR was willing to sell the rifles and ammunition that had been manufactured for the German army in Czechoslovakia during WWII and were still stored there. Purchase of these arms was really a lifesaver for the newly established State of Israel."

The explanation was helpful but it took quite a while for me to get to feel comfortable with the Nazi insignia on my rifle. Eventually, I made friends with it as I learned to clean it and take care of it, as a good soldier must. I found that the weapon functioned well for me and I turned out to be a reasonable marksman when we were taken to the practice range. This was the only time in my life that I fired a weapon.

I never did find out for sure why the Soviets decided to sell arms to Israel. One possible and simple explanation is that they wanted the hard currency they received in payment. The only other reasonable, but unsubstantiated, explanation I have found goes like this: At the time, the Arab countries were probably considered to be too religious to be accessible to Soviet influence. On the other hand, the government of the new Jewish state was known to have a socialist orientation and the USSR may have believed that it might be able to exert influence in the Middle East via this avenue. We know that this never came to pass since Israel was strongly tied to the West, while the Arab countries, led by Egypt under Abdul Nasser soon allied themselves with the Soviets. The Czech rifle survived for quite a few years in the Israeli army and my daughters also were issued this weapon when they returned to Israel to do their army service in the 1970s. However, by then the swastika markings had been shaved off.

In due course, I came to understand that President Truman was the first to recognize the State of Israel but he did not lift the arms embargo, and Israel was left to solve its problem of self-defense by itself!

I had been inducted into the army reserves after having arrived in Haifa from Berkeley in October 1952, and had begun teaching.

I had received an order to attend a month's training course as *Mishne Techni,* which turned out to be a technician in the artillery. In those days, long before computers and even before hand-held calculators came to be in general use, calculations for aiming guns had to be made using logarithmic and trigonometric tables, all of which I was well-acquainted with from my science education. It did not come as a surprise to me that I excelled on the tests we were given and one instructor, who later enrolled in an engineering course at the Technion, wrote in large letters *Yofi,* meaning beautiful, on such a test. I was later amused when a well-meaning sergeant told the group how, in a more advanced course, we would be taught the use of the slide rule, another dinosaur of a tool dating to an earlier age.

Towards the end of the artillery technicians' course, the commander, a captain in the regular army, made a momentous announcement at the morning roll call.

"I have decided to take you all out on maneuvers in the Latrun sector. We have conducted a parallel course for heavy caliber howitzer crews and they will join in these maneuvers. You will be assigned to performing the calculations necessary for aiming the guns and to man lookout positions to monitor the fire. They will fire the guns using live ammunition. A high order of discipline will be required to prevent casualties. I wish you all success!"

All of us were gripped by excitement after hearing the commander's announcement and we worked hard and with increased dedication to prepare ourselves for the maneuvers. During those days, it was repeatedly impressed on us that we were now to show that we were indeed ready to take on the challenge and needed to be focused. We took our exercises more seriously now that we anticipated a realistic situation.

Otto Schnepp

We finally mounted the trucks and followed the commander who rode in an armored personnel carrier, followed by the battery of howitzers of French manufacture. On arrival at the designated site for the battery's emplacements, the guns were positioned; I did my calculations and called out the required settings to the gun crew that I was assigned to. **And the guns boomed! And they boomed again and again!**

It is hard to describe the effect of the boom of the guns on me. It was as if I had swallowed a belly full of comfort food and could now walk more erect and with a confidence I had never felt before. The memory, 60 years later, still brings tears to my eyes as I recall the experience. A primitive reaction, all right — but for that reason, all the more deeply emotional. If I were to fix on a moment when my recovery from trauma began, this was it.

At the time I was not that clear about my reaction and its cause. I simply was not that much in touch with my feelings and inner process. But I knew that the guns' booms felt mighty good. It took many years of therapy and self-exploration before I recovered my full range of human feelings, which I had repressed for so long.

Chapter 14

Tragedy Strikes

"Otto!" I looked in the direction of the voice and saw one of the graduate students holding the receiver of the only telephone located at the other end of the hallway.

"Otto, it is for you," he called out.

It was my mother's landlord.

"You better go to the Rothschild Hospital. The ambulance took your mother there. Something has happened."

"What happened?" was my first automatic response.

"Go there," the voice at the other end just repeated, implying finality.

Since I did not have a car at the time, I went to the bus station, but a *sherut* (a jitney taxi) came first and picked me up. As I sank into my seat and the taxi followed the winding road up Mt. Carmel in Haifa, I reflected on the cryptic message. I became aware of the anxiety creeping up my spine. Mother had suffered from bouts of depression and had been hospitalized after a suicide attempt (cutting her wrist) two years before. She had received electric shock treatments at the mental hospital to pull her out of depression.

The mental hospital was located in a fortress originally built by the Ottoman Turks in the ancient city of Ako (Acre) that lies across the bay from Haifa, which has been known as a port since ancient times. The Crusaders landed there on their way to Jerusalem and Napoleon fought a battle to capture it. It had been used as a prison by the British Government under the Mandate of the United Nations of Palestine right up to the establishment of the State of Israel in 1948, Jewish freedom fighters (or terrorists) were imprisoned there, and some of them were actually executed there. The place sent shivers down my spine when I visited Mother while she was hospitalized there and when I had to take her for shock treatments as an outpatient afterwards. It was in a state of partial demolition really, more like an ancient ruin from Crusader times, than a comforting site suitable for healing souls. It reminded me of the "snake pit" — a mental hospital of some 100-200 years ago. But this was 1955!

Mother had been suffering from another depression and was again receiving shock treatments on an outpatient basis. She had shown signs of improvement, and the night before, I had brought her by bus to our house where we had had dinner and spent some pleasant time together. Mother seemed to particularly enjoy interacting with our first daughter, who was just short of two years old and had learned to call her "Ganny."

Just before mother left, she said: "I am such a burden to you."

And I had responded, "We enjoy watching you play with Debbie."

She did not reply, and I was not sure she was encouraged by my remark. I had accompanied her home by bus.

As I sat in the taxi, I prepared myself for finding Mother after another suicide attempt. The Rothschild Hospital was the hospital of the Haifa municipality, a modern structure near the peak of Mt. Carmel. At the ER, they called a doctor to speak to me. He seemed hesitant and spoke in an accented German — obviously a new immigrant, probably from Poland. There had recently been a wave of immigration from Poland, which decided to allow Jews to leave — an exceptional decision by a Soviet-dominated country.

"Your mother was brought here by ambulance. Unfortunately, we could only determine that she had expired. She has a wound on her neck. The police have been notified, and they will arrive shortly. They will probably want to speak with you."

Two policemen soon drove up in a jeep, and one of them, whom I presumed to be the senior officer, led the conversation.

"We need to obtain information from you concerning your mother's recent history of physical and mental health. But first I want to explain that the doctor has certified that your mother bled to death as a result of a cut on her neck that severed a major artery. It is our task to investigate the circumstances of her death in order to determine if any criminal act has been committed. We have already visited your mother's residence and have recovered a blood-stained razor blade from her bed. We have also interviewed the landlord who heard moaning noises from her room and then called the ambulance."

It was now my turn to report what I knew. They then asked me to identify my mother. I was shown into a bare room where my mother's body was lying on a table. It was an eerie experience. I had only once been in the presence of corpses, piles of them, after an aerial bombardment by U.S. planes close to the end of the war in Shanghai in the summer of 1945. They uncovered mother's face. I shuddered with feelings of horror and repulsion when I saw the face with the skin pulled tightly over the cheek-bones. I managed to nod in assent. Then they took me by car to mother's residence nearby.

We entered the small apartment. There was blood on the bed, on the walls, everywhere I looked. More horror!

One of the policemen told me: "The place must be cleaned up very soon, otherwise a strong stench will infest the apartment, and will be very difficult to get rid of later!"

The policemen took me to my home, and I gave Miriam the news. I also tried to phone my sister Herta, who lived at the time in Nairobi, Kenya. That was really difficult since there was only one phone in the entire block of about twelve prefab houses erected by the Technion-Israel Institute of Technology for new faculty from abroad, and that phone was outside. I did finally get Herta on the line, but the connection was very noisy.

I shouted, "Mother committed suicide! This time she succeeded after all the previous attempts!"

This was not the kind of news I wanted to broadcast to the entire neighborhood. I would have preferred to have an intimate conversation with my sister. I finally gave up on the phone and settled for a good old-fashioned cable from the post office.

Mother had had a long history of pessimism foreshadowing depression. I remember her alluding to it when I was a child of perhaps ten.

"Sometimes I see only black," she said to somebody in my presence and this memory stuck in my mind. Only much later did I realize the significance of her remark. She was, however, a good mother to me, and gave me a lot of love and affection.

Mother's first wrist-cutting suicide attempt took place in Herta's house where she had brought Mother to live after Father's recent death. Herta was terrified to keep her there for fear that her children would one day find her in such a state. Herta had

Mother taken to a local sanatorium. and then, when she had recovered sufficiently and my wife, Miriam and I had arrived in Israel from Berkeley, Mother came to join us. At first she stayed with us in our limited apartment, but after some time, we managed to find the one-room accommodation where she could live independently.

I went through the motions of talking to the policemen and identifying Mother's body in a near-robotic state. When I finally had time to sit down and think I realized that I was emotionally conflicted. It was of course sad that mother had obviously suffered during her episodes of depression and that she had died a violent death by her own hand, which testified to the extreme desperation she must have felt. On the other hand, her death was also a relief for Miriam and me and perhaps also for herself. When I had taken Mother for shock treatments as an outpatient, I never witnessed these treatments, but I imagined the procedure to be cruel and thoroughly unnatural. I actually felt physical and emotional pain while waiting for two hours or so until she recovered from the treatment and I could take her home. I also sometimes even felt anger towards Mother for imposing this problem on us as we struggled to settle into a new and strange environment. I had not grasped the seriousness of her disease.

The next task was to get the apartment cleaned up. I could not think of anybody whom I could get to do this and was embarrassed to ask for help. I finally went there and did it by myself. This was a real ordeal and I felt immersed in the entire violent act of mother's suicide. My body resisted, and I had to push myself to keep going. It took several hours. I also felt remorse. "I should have taken better care of her" was one thought with which I tortured myself. I was not yet ready at the time to accept that I had been powerless in the face of this terrible and finally fatal disease that had plagued Mother for many years.

I could not eat tomatoes for a long time. The color took me back to the blood-stained apartment and shook me up every time I tried. However, time passed, and I recovered from this painful experience.

In accordance with Jewish practice, and in Israel, the orthodox religious laws prevail and are imposed on all Jewish residents to this day — the funeral had to take place within twenty-four hours. I was warned to wear an old jacket because the official conducting the burial would slice a deep cut in my lapel as a symbol of mourning. Fortunately, a very nice man (Otto Stiefel was his name) who was the driver of the station wagon owned by the Technion, took charge, drove us to the cemetery and got me through the ordeal of the proceedings. There were not enough men at the graveside to say the "Kadish" — ten men or a "minyan" is required for prayer — and I was told that I would have to attend a service at a synagogue. I refrained from following that instruction. Religious observances were not part of my life and, in particular, I rejected the imposition of Orthodox Jewish tradition on the private lives of all Jewish residents of Israel. At least, they did not drag me to the synagogue by force!

Some weeks after Mother's death I shared my feelings with Miriam:

"You know, I must confess that I feel as if I have been liberated from a dark shadow that has hovered over my life during recent years. It is time to plan for the future. I want to spend a year or two abroad. It will be good for us to put some distance between us and the events surrounding Mother's depression

Chapter 15

Rise and Fall

"You will have to take over as department head. Kurt has alienated many people, and I hope that he will not be reelected. I will go on sabbatical leave beginning in the fall, and you are the best candidate. I will use my influence to support you."

David and I habitually conversed in English when alone. He was American and had attended schools in Palestine before the establishment of the State of Israel. His Hebrew was very close to being on the "native speaker" level, but he retained a distinct American accent. We were faculty at the Israel Institute of Technology, or Technion for short, in Haifa.

David's words sent shivers down my spine. My immediate reaction was ambivalent. There was fear and excitement: fear of the responsibility I was asked to assume and excitement over the recognition of me as a leader of the department. His selection of me as his favorite candidate for becoming department head in his absence was like a shot of stimulant setting my heart aquiver. I was all of 34 years old.

David commanded a great deal of respect among the faculty members of the department, as well as broadly in the institution. He had transferred from the Weitzman Institute and had taken over the Chemistry Department. It was his influence with the administration that had created the budgetary and physical conditions required for productive research.

I consulted my close friend Pinhas, who was not in the department.

"What do you think of all this?" I asked. "Can I really lead this department? True, we are mostly young scientists, but I do not feel sure of my ability to act as their leader. I lack the administrative experience and the ability to take charge of a group of 25 faculty members and persuade or cajole them to agree on reasonable decisions."

Examples of decisions in question concerned teaching programs, new appointments, promotions and tenure.

"You will need to give the group a lot of time to discuss and listen to each other before you can expect agreement on any issue," Pinhas responded. He continued: "Actually, I don't see that you have much of a choice. If David considers you to be the best candidate, you will have to take up the challenge and run with it!"

I also had a conversation with Dov, a member of the department with close personal ties to David.

"Look, if David will prepare the ground as he promised, you will have the support of many of us," Dov said.

Two months later after talking individually to many of my colleagues, I still harbored a lot of doubt and trepidation. We met to elect the department head for the next term, and I received a large majority with only two votes for Kurt. A group of us went to celebrate at the Haifa Theatre Club where a then unknown young actor, called Chaim Topol, played a leading role in many of the skits. Topol was to become a star in the successful film, *Fiddler on the Roof.*

Things went pretty well for a while. David had urged me:

"Be sure to fire the departmental secretary appointed by Kurt before she is eligible for tenure!"

I had little hesitation in following David's advice (or better, his instruction) since I needed a secretary who was good at Hebrew, a skill required for the administration of the department and internal Israeli correspondence. The incumbent was a recent immigrant from America who did not fill this bill. It was difficult for me to carry out the dismissal, particularly when Kurt came to argue in her favor. I steeled myself and held steady. The real problem was, however, that I did not find the candidates sent to me for interviews for the job by the senior administrative officer to be satisfactory. Soon pressure mounted on me to resolve the problem. Fortunately, Dvorah, the secretary for the section of physical chemistry, with whom I had worked for two years, was a qualified and willing source of support.

"Dvorah, you will have to help me manage the departmental office until I find somebody suitable to fill the job," I told her.

"I will do my best — you can count on me," was Dvorah's response.

Then, one day, the administration sent me Kochava (Hebrew for female star)! She was smart, effective and experienced, and she was good-looking to boot. She stayed in the job for the next 25 years until her retirement. My perseverance had paid off.

My appointment as department head was for two years. The first year David was abroad in the United States, and he would send me "suggestions" on various policy issues.

"Be sure to get approval for this appointment" and "talk to Shlomo before you announce this decision" or "don't allow other faculty members to sway you — stick to this decision!"

One day, my patience wore thin, and I wrote to David:

"Look, if you want to run the department, why don't you come back and take charge?"

I fully realize in retrospect that this was not the best idea, but I was young and headstrong and had not yet matured to the wisdom of being diplomatic. My message was clear: You put me here in this position and now, please treat me accordingly. Colleagues advised me to adopt a different tone, and I did.

"David, I shall try my best but I cannot promise to always be able to deliver an outcome that will be to your satisfaction."

That worked better. He responded:

"I understand this, but still, I encourage you to try this approach."

After a year, David returned and was appointed Acting Director of the Technion while the permanent Director, Rav Aluf (Lieutenant General and former Chief of Staff) Ya'akov Dori took a leave of absence to rest and to recuperate from some chronic ailment. I tried to keep at a distance from David, but was not always successful. Nevertheless, our relations were cordial but a bit formal, including our conversing in Hebrew. I suppose that this was reasonable under the circumstances. He was now the Director and had to keep some distance between himself and the staff.

After this second year of being department head, I planned to get back to full-time teaching and research. I was definitely feeling that my work with my graduate students had suffered and I, myself, worked 70 to 80-hour weeks to keep all aspects of my work going. There was the administrative and personnel management, staffing of the teaching program, constant consultations with faculty members, a myriad of things to be taken care of and, finally, my research including the supervision of five doctoral students.

I also had become aware that I was neglecting my family although I insisted on reserving the Shabat (Sabbath; in Israel, this is Saturday for the Jewish community) for activities with my wife and two daughters, Debbie and Judy.

"Let us plan for a nice outing this Shabat," I said to Miriam one day.

"Let's see what the weather will be like. Actually, I don't really enjoy these long car rides so much. I also hate getting out and walking in this heat," Miriam responded.

"Come on now, the children always enjoy our trips to the Galilee, to Zfat (Safed) or the Kinneret (Sea of Galilee)," I said. "Come, let's do this. I also want to have a chance to spend time with the children, and they like to go on walks in these places. If you don't want to hike, you can find some place to sit and read. During our drives, the girls and I have a lot of fun singing. Debbie knows a lot of songs that she can teach us."

"I don't know — you could just take the girls for a walk right nearby on Mt. Carmel. There is no need to go so far," Miriam insisted. She was in her discouraging mode and needed to be coaxed a bit more.

"Really, it is good to go somewhere and explore. It is good for the girls to get out into the countryside. My mother gave me this gift — a love for nature, and it has been a benefit and a source of pleasure. Come, make an effort, and you will be glad for it. We will have a lot of fun!"

"O.K., if it has to be," Miriam conceded and her voice conveyed her reluctance. "Let's go to Lake Kinneret. I like the peaceful atmosphere of Capernaum."

Capernaum is, indeed, a place on the shore of the lake, that conveys calm and serenity. I always liked Capernaum; it is a significant place for me. The ancient remains of the building stones with designs carved into them are remnants of the synagogue where tradition has it that Christ preached. The place signifies the confluence of the two religions, Judaism and Christianity.

At other times, we joined friends on hikes on Mt. Carmel or in the Galilee.

ROOTS LOST-ROOTS FOUND

"Nick is leading the hike tomorrow to Montfort, the remains of the Crusader castle in the Upper Galilee," I proclaimed with enthusiasm on coming home from the Technion one Friday afternoon.

"Great, I love to go on hikes with the Kleins and the Oppenheims and their children," Debbie responded.

The children had a good time climbing around the ruins of the castle, even though it took well over an hour's walk to get there from the road along sometimes difficult paths.

In the summer, we spent many weekend days at the wonderful beaches of Northern Israel, swimming and playing ball games.

During the second year of my tenure as department head, I began to sense that I had accumulated a significant dose of resentment among the members of my department in reaction to my decision-making. As everyone in a position of authority sooner or later finds out, I did not succeed in satisfying everybody all the time. In retrospect, I believe that I was young and did not have enough stature or prestige to compensate for stepping on some toes.

As the two years were coming to a close, David asked me to come to his office.

"You have done a creditable job as department head," David began. "I am now concluding my year as Director of the Institute and need a rest. I also want to attend to my academic activities, and, as you now know, administration does, eventually, interfere. I believe it would be good for the department and also for yourself if you were to continue as department head for a third year. You have enough experience to realize, I am sure, that administration has its rewards, and it is difficult to see programs mature and show results after a short tenure. What do you say?"

David used English to convey informality, and to be more persuasive, I suspect.

"Give me some time to think it over," I responded, not wanting to commit myself and looking for some breathing space in which to come to a reasoned decision.

I was not enthused by the prospect of another pressured year, but I also was gratified by David's implied approval. I discussed my situation with Miriam.

"David has asked me to continue as department head for a third year. I am flattered by his approval and support and am tempted to accept his offer. On the other hand, it has been a strain to keep up with the demands on my time. I really need to spend more of my energy on my science and teaching. After all, this is what has real value. I fear that the tension in me affects my interpersonal relations, including those with you and the children. Often, I feel pressured, and I am aware that I react with impatience."

"I have certainly felt that you are under pressure and often are impatient. I could do with more patience and attention from you and you must spend more time with the children and me. It is high time that you got out of this job!" Miriam responded.

This conversation supported me in standing fast and resisting David's urging to continue as department head for a third year.

David persisted for a while in pushing me, sometimes subtly and at other times not so subtly, but after some additional tussles, it became clear to him that I was resolved to terminate my tenure as department head. Eventually another department head was recruited by the intervention of no less a personality than General Dori. This is the way Dov described to me what had happened:

"Look, Dori came to my house and asked me to accept the position of department head. There was no way I could refuse him!"

Dov originally was a strong supporter of mine, but I was to learn that he resented being placed in the position of having no way out, and, as a result he also did not look kindly on my refusal to stay in the job. In the process, I also incurred the disfavor of David for refusing to accede to his request, so that he was put in the position of having to ask the General himself to help him get his way with his own home department faculty.

During the year of David's tenure as acting director, he arranged for a visit by David Ben Gurion to the institution, and I got to shake the hand of the fabled leader and founder of the State of Israel on this occasion. David derived a significant dose of visibility from this visit and was also instrumental in changing the title of the head of the Technion from director to president. I suspect that David really hoped that General Dori would not return after his year of leave and would retire. Then, David would have been in a good position to be appointed president himself, or so he may have thought. However, I believe that many possibilities were flowing, some in confluence and others at crosscurrents.

"I have heard from many faculty members that they are wary of David's ambitions, and they would resist a power grab by him," my friend Pinhas told me at the time.

Evidently there were higher stakes at play than my struggles, which only played out in the ripples at the margins of the maelstrom.

During the following year, I successfully got my research work going full speed again and kept myself out of departmental affairs, except that I continued to have responsibility for the coordination of the physical chemistry section. One day, David asked me to go for a cup of coffee with him.

"I believe that it is time for others in the physical chemistry section to participate and take the lead. Both Mordachai and Reuben have matured sufficiently to take over more responsibility and to relieve you. I have decided to recommend to Dov that he appoint Reuben as coordinator of physical chemistry."

The message was clear. David, who was now back in the department, aimed at sidelining me in the departmental power structure. I had demonstrated more independence of mind than he wanted to have to deal with, I suspect. He evidently felt challenged by me in his position of "primus inter pares" in the department (as it is often said: "all are equal but some are more equal.")

I felt the change of my position as an emotional crisis — not major, but significant. Rotation of administrative responsibility among faculty members in an academic unit should be seen and accepted as routine and almost always is in academia — at least that has been my experience. This case was not different on the surface, but it all happened in an atmosphere of tensions exacerbated by David's wish to stay in control. At least this is how I saw it. Also, his strategy was transparent. Reuben was a mild personality and was clearly unsuited for a position of administration and leadership. He was evidently to provide for a smooth transition on the strength that he would not evoke controversy. Mordechai was appointed to succeed Reuben after a year.

I immersed myself in my teaching and research and had no difficulty in maintaining my good personal relations with Reuben and Mordechai, both of whom sought my advice and treated me with respect.

ROOTS LOST-ROOTS FOUND

David took over the departmental chairmanship after Dov concluded his two years at the helm. It became clear to me that David intentionally excluded me from discussions of departmental affairs, which were often carried out in small informal groups. I heard that decisions had been made without anyone letting me know about it or worrying about my being informed of the meetings. Of course, this arrangement also had a bright side. It saved me time that I could put to better use than spending it on discussions that, by their very nature, are inefficient in terms of time spent. Nevertheless, I was outside the circuit and it did rankle. Years later the departmental secretary, Kochava, by then retired from the job, sought to meet with me and told me that she was aware of my being isolated at the time and had pointed it out to David. It was good to know that all this was not just a manifestation of my paranoia.

I felt increasingly uneasy and was ready for a change.

Chapter 16

Otto The Diplomat
Part 1

I was attending a scientific conference in 1979 and having lunch with several colleagues. George turned to me and out of the blue said: "Otto, how would you like to go to China for two years?"

And that was the beginning of a grand adventure.

"What is this all about, George?" I responded after having recovered from my surprise.

I knew that George, a prominent Professor of Chemistry at UC Berkeley, was at the time serving a limited term as Deputy Director of the National Science Foundation (NSF) in Washington, but I had no idea what he was talking about. After lunch he asked me to sit down with him in a more private place, and he gave me a short overview of the background of his question.

"In my present position at NSF I have had contact with a number of cooperative international scientific programs run by the State Department and various federal agencies. I know that the China desk at the State Department and the Office of Science and Technology Policy are looking for an appropriately qualified person, ideally someone with China background, and I think it important to appoint someone with scientific credentials. The current Scientific Advisor to President Jimmy Carter, Frank Press, is a well-known geophysicist and the director of the Office of Science and Technology Policy. He is taking a special interest in this appointment and supports my idea of the required qualifications for it. I believe that you are the best possible candidate and I urge you to give serious consideration to the proposed two-year appointment as Science Attaché to launch the program on Science and Technology at the U.S. Embassy in Beijing, which was established only a year ago."

After a lot of thought, and having gotten over the first burst of excitement, I settled down to seriously weigh the pros and cons of this unexpected opportunity. It would be a new experience to explore the mysterious workings of an Embassy, particularly in a country that had been closed to Americans for thirty years, since the establishment of the People's Republic of China under Mao Zedong in 1949.

On a personal level, I decided that it was a good time to take off some time from my academic work. In a sense I was just going through a kind of midlife crisis and had lost some of the edge of my ambition to forge ahead; this was the result of a personal experience with psychotherapy and a divorce from my first wife, Miriam, after a 24-year marriage. I decided to pursue the opportunity to spend two years as a foreign service officer posted to the U.S. Embassy in Beijing; I had even begun to tune in to the official language.

The first step was getting a security clearance processed by the Security Service of the State Department for the China desk. This turned out to be a complicated procedure for which I had to fill out a daunting pile of forms, describing and documenting my personal history and listing all travel abroad. The latter was most challenging since I have lived in and been a citizen of Austria and Israel with extended interspersed stays in Shanghai and the United States. The U.S. Government is a large and complex organization and many people had to review my application and approve it or "sign off" as they say in the accepted lingo. I was interviewed at length by an official at the office of the Security Service in Los Angeles, and I visited the State Department in Washington where I went through a series of interviews, reaching as high as an Undersecretary. The official description of my position during the first year was to be Attaché for Science and Technology in the Foreign Service.

I felt it advisable to brush up on my knowledge of Chinese. Fortunately, I had been stimulated by President Nixon's visit to China in 1972, accompanied by his Security Advisor and later Secretary of State, Henry Kissinger. At that time he reestablished a low level of diplomatic relations between the countries, and the U.S. opened a Liaison Office in Beijing. The front page of the *Los Angeles Times* reproduced an image of the front page of the *People's Daily* and I decided to review my knowledge of Chinese with the help of a graduate student in the Chemistry Department at USC, where I was a faculty member.

That experience gave me some self- assurance quickly.

Another wrinkle was my personal life. At the time I was living with Judith and we had to work out our relationship status. [See Chapter 19 for more information about the women in my life.] After some back and forth tussles, Judith decided that she would join me on this China adventure and we also thought it best to get married, at least for the two-year period of our planned stay in Beijing. Another hurdle then surfaced: Judith was a long-term resident of the United States but had retained her British citizenship. We assumed that we would be better off with her getting naturalized, and even that was accomplished before we had to leave for China. There was enough time to complete all these procedures since my security clearance and the ambassador's consent for my joining the Embassy, including living quarters and office space in Beijing, had to be arranged for. I asked for, and obtained, a two year-leave of absence from the university. Eventually, all the required papers were ready for my taking up my position in Beijing and the necessary "orders were cut" — to use the official language — for our leaving in August 1980. The State Department encouraged foreign service officers going to China to bring a car, and I was advised that Toyota had a maintenance service garage in Beijing. Accordingly, I purchased a new Toyota Corona. I rented out my house in Los Angeles, and the State Department arranged for movers to empty it out. With the guidance of the State Department we designated part of the contents, furniture and all, for storage, another part for our use in China to be sent by ship, and a smaller third part, more urgently needed to begin our new life, to be sent to Beijing by air.

My first assignment in the Foreign Service was to travel to Washington for a two-week orientation under the guidance of the China Desk and the Office of Science and Technology Policy. This consisted of a series of visits to federal agencies which I was to represent in Beijing, including the National Oceanic and Atmospheric Agency (NOAA), U.S. Geological Survey (USGS) (including Seismology), National Science Foundation (NSF), Food and Drug Administration (FDA), Pentagon, State Department Bureau of Intelligence, and inevitably the CIA.

One day during my orientation program in Washington, the assistant to Frank Press, the President's Science Advisor, who oversaw this program, called me in and told me:

"There happens to be a visiting Chinese S&T delegation in town and I believe you should meet with them. It is a good opportunity to announce your appointment to them and to introduce you to Chinese S&T officials. I will arrange your meeting with them."

There were about ten members of this delegation led by a Vice Minister of the Science and Technology Commission (STC). The Chinese at that time considered it a priority to take advantage of any opportunity to benefit from interactions with American scientists after their long period of isolation following the establishment of the People's Republic of China (PRC) in 1949 and during the so-called Cultural Revolution of 1965, until the death of Chairman Mao in 1976. The cooperative S&T activities with the United States under an agreement signed by the new dynamic leader Deng Xiaoping during his historic visit to the U.S. in January 1979 was the starting bell for China's opening up. My appointment was central to this program, since I soon came to realize that overseeing its implementation constituted approximately half of my job description.

Otto Schnepp

My meeting with the Chinese S&T delegation was a great success. When I introduced myself as a graduate of St. John's University in Shanghai, it was as if the whole room came alive. Inevitably, one of the group was from Shanghai and he challenged me, in the local dialect, if I spoke it. I let loose with a sentence or two and was roundly applauded.

I thought it was important to spread the word of my appointment within the U.S. science community and made arrangements to meet with the best-known ethnic Chinese scientists, who coincidentally had visited China early on in the 1970s following Nixon's opening up of the relationship between the countries. There were three Nobel Laureates among those: T.D. Lee and C.N. Yang who were professors at Columbia University and had shared the Nobel Prize in Physics 1957. I made successful contact with Lee, who was spending the summer at the Brookhaven National Laboratory on Long Island; my appointment to the Beijing embassy opened the door and he was amenable to seeing me and filling me in on his view of the state of science in China. Yang was out of the country, but I did visit a prominent Chinese American woman professor at Columbia, C.S. Wu, who very graciously invited me for lunch at the university, and shared with me her recent experiences in China, including her view of the new leader, Deng Xiaoping. I remember her quoting him as getting up in the middle of a meal he hosted in her honor and muttering to himself, "so many people, so many people!" Wu was a very prominent physics professor who performed the experiment which confirmed the predictions of the theory of physical parity proposed by Lee and Yang and their Nobel Prize was awarded based on Wu's experimental results.

When I finally arrived in Beijing, the host agency, the Science and Technology Commission (STC), knew of me and I was warmly welcomed. This is not to say that they laid aside their suspicion that I might well be a CIA agent, but then it was of course true that I was there also to report back on the state of S&T in the laboratories and research institutes that I was allowed to visit.

Here is a brief explanation of the term "physical parity."

"For a long time physicists had assumed that different types of symmetries characterize nature. In a kind of mirror-world, the physical laws should be the same if right and left are exchanged and if matter is replaced by antimatter. However, for certain decays of elementary particles the equality of the laws was questioned, and Tsung Dao Lee and Chen Ning Yang formulated in 1956 a theory stating that the left-right symmetry law is violated for the weak interaction. Measurements (by C.S. Wu) of the decay electrons from a cobalt isotope confirmed the symmetry violation."

At a meeting of the China Committee of the National Academy of Sciences and also later in Pasadena where he was visiting at the California Institute of Technology, I met another bright light on the firmament, MIT physics professor, Samuel C.C. Ting (Ding) who shared the prize with an American physicist at Stanford in 1976, The China Committee sponsored a number of groups of American scholars who visited China early on and whose reports I studied: one a group of chemists and another of historians. I also remember being intrigued by the report of a group that investigated the success of acupuncture.

I met again with Lee and Ting during my stay in Beijing. T.D. Lee (often referred to as TD) occupies a special lofty place among physicists. In the course of one of his visits to China during my tenure at the embassy, TD asked me to attend a meeting he had arranged, but I said I had a previous commitment that day. A prominent American physicist witnessed the interchange between TD and me and, in private, he admonished me:

"You may cross your ambassador, but **never cross** TD!"

I rearranged my schedule and did as TD had requested.

After a short stay in Honolulu, Judith and I proceeded to Beijing with another short stay in Tokyo (from Chapter 16-2 — slight variation combined with 16-1). Traveling on a diplomatic passport brings a valuable privilege: a fast line through Customs and Passport Control. A Foreign Service officer of the Embassy's Economic Section met us and took us in an embassy car into the city to the Beijing Hotel which, at the time (August 1980) was the only hotel where foreigners could stay. We passed through the gate on the strength of the diplomatic license plate of the car, I later found out. The hotel was surrounded by an ironwork fence through which curious Chinese stared at all foreigners coming and going. It felt rather like we were in a cage and exhibited for view.

This took some getting used to. At the time, there were few foreigners in China and the proximity of the Beijing Central Railroad Station caused travelers waiting for their trains to entertain themselves by foreigner-watching.

We settled into a good-sized room with a bathroom and were told that it would probably take a few months before we would be able to move into an apartment. We met the Commercial Counselor, my boss for the first year, and I had appointments with the Ambassador, Leonard Woodcock, and the Deputy Chief of Mission (DCM), J. Stapleton Roy, the next day at the embassy where I was taken by an embassy car. Woodcock had been appointed the first Ambassador to China by President Carter and had negotiated the terms of the mutual full recognition with the Chinese Government. He had been the president of the Auto Workers Union and I had heard that he was thought qualified as a successful negotiator on the strength of his record of achievements in negotiations with the Big Three (Ford, GM and Chrysler). A Doonesbury cartoon at the time read, "If he can take on the Big Three, he can handle the Gang of Four."

ROOTS LOST-ROOTS FOUND

Woodcock was a rather taciturn man and he only muttered some formal words of welcome: "Welcome to Beijing. We hope that we can find an apartment for you soon. You will have to make the best of it at the Beijing Hotel, meanwhile."

Roy (informally called Stape), on the other hand, was friendly and open. He got up, shook my hand and, after inviting me to sit down, expressed interest in my personal background.

"Good to see you here, finally. I am sorry it took longer than expected to get you and your wife cleared. We need you here and there is a lot of work to be done. You can count on my support. I want to make an effort to push the S&T cooperation with China forward. The Chinese government under Deng Xiaoping is eager to get as much training as possible out of us. Let's see what we can do! We will work on getting you settled in an apartment soon and I hope to provide you with the support you will need for your work here. I want you to attend the weekly staff meetings of Counselors and others will understand that you have a special position at the embassy."

The DCM administers the embassy and under him the heads of the various sections — political, commercial, cultural, consular, etc. - are each headed by a Counselor.

I was buoyed by Roy's promise of support and his interest in my mission. He clearly was a highly-educated man who was reputed to have deep knowledge of Chinese language and literature, and he appreciated my qualifications. This turned out to be important since I soon found out that the career foreign service staff viewed me with suspicion. I was an outsider, planted in their midst, and I also was not a "youngster who could be kicked around" in the non-diplomatic words of my immediate boss, the Commercial Counselor. He evidently said this with some regret. In fact, I was given the next-to highest rank in the Foreign Service Reserve bureaucracy (FSR-2). Roy (or Stape) after several intermediate appointments in East Asia returned to Beijing as Ambassador during 1991-95.

Most of Roy's tenure as Ambassador was during President Bill Clinton's term of office (1993-2001). However, President George H.W. Bush appointed him. Ambassador Woodcock left office in February 1981, soon after the election of President Reagan who defeated President Jimmy Carter in November 1980. There was a period of several months before the next Ambassador, Arthur W. Hummel, took up his post and in the interim the DCM, Stape (Roy), was the chargé d'affaires, acting as head of the embassy.

My first experience after arrival at the embassy was a short plane trip to Dalian (also known as Dairen and adjacent Port Arthur during the Russo-Japanese war, 1904-05) in Manchuria (the northeast part of China), the location of the Dalian University of Technology. I accompanied the ambassador to the opening of a six-months business school course for Chinese managers organized by the U.S. Department of Commerce under the Science & Technology (S&T) agreement in cooperation with the People's Republic of China (PRC) S&T Commission (STC), which recruited the students. This was the first significant activity under this agreement and there were the required speeches in Chinese and English with translations. I was to monitor this course, which was to be repeated several times over the following few years. It was a good opportunity to get acquainted with the faculty, which had been recruited from a number of business schools in the United States, and with whom I met again during follow-up trips. I also met a minister of the STC with whom I had many encounters in Beijing during my stay, and an official who acted as his assistant and interpreter, Li Mingde.

I soon began my visits to the various research institutes of the Academy of Sciences and institutions of higher learning throughout China, all arranged at my request by the STC and facilitated by Li. As a result, I had the opportunity to inspect the scientific equipment in these laboratories; this was 1980 and it was clear that the instrumentation was of 1950s vintage. Much had changed in the intervening thirty years in laboratories in the U.S. with the introduction of automation based on solid-state electronics.

When I traveled out-of-town, by air mostly, I was able to take Judith along. She welcomed these occasions and the institutions I visited were hospitable and arranged for her to have tours of the cities and visits to monuments and temples while I was busy. On weekends, I participated in such tours but I believe that Judith saw more of China than I did. In Beijing, Judith took lessons in Chinese and participated in Tai Chi (taijiquan) classes where she met a number of ambassadors and other interesting members of the international community. We also went to see dance performances and we saw a variety of

Chinese opera programs. These were good introductions to Chinese culture, particularly when we could find explanatory materials to read in advance of attending the performances. We drew on the help from the Cultural Section of the embassy, whose staff was well-educated and were a good source of reading material.

I remember once Judith asking the cultural counselor how long it takes to learn Chinese. His reply was: "The first ten years are the hardest." Not very encouraging, I thought. Fortunately, I had gained my basic knowledge of Chinese when I was young and learning was a lot easier.

Chapter 17

Otto The Diplomat Part 2

There were many visiting delegations repre-
senting U.S. agencies that partnered in activities under the Science & Technology (S&T)
Agreement. During the day there were joint meetings discussing and negotiating the details of the
plans for cooperative activities and visits to Chinese
institutions. In the evening there were banquets
hosted by the Chinese partner agencies. It became a
routine for me to attend these meetings and banquets since the U.S. partners relied on me to assist
and advise around the formalities such as toasts
with declarations of friendship. The Chinese hosts
always provided interpreters to bridge the language
barriers between the leaders of the delegations. It

was my job, for example, to explain that the banquets were scheduled to begin at 6 p.m. and lasted exactly two hours. At 8 p.m. the Chinese host got up and it was time to go through the parting ceremonies. I often returned to the embassy to work in spite of having participated in toasts, drinking shot glass size portions of a distilled drink, *Mao Tai*, which is made from fermented sorghum and is 144 proof in alcohol content. I usually was able to work after three such drinks, but no more. After that my legs felt heavy and my head shut down.

During joint sessions negotiating detailed plans of the cooperative programs, I found it useful to monitor the Chinese interpreters' translation of sums of money. Mistakes arise from the Chinese numbering system using a unit of 10,000, called *wan*. Interpreters under time pressure often translated the *wan* as a million whereas a million is 100 *wan*.

Gérard was the science counselor at the French Embassy in Beijing. I discovered that he was the first cousin of old friends of mine from Shanghai and we had a great collaborative relationship. At the time, in the beginning of the 1980s we were both occupied with the potential sale to China of a nuclear electric power reactor to be installed in Canton province, just outside Hong Kong, to supply power to Hong Kong and the entire region. Financial support came from the Kadoories, a Sephardic Jewish family of financiers and philanthropists, who had been prominent in Shanghai before Pearl Harbor.

"So, which one of us will win this race, France or the U.S.?" Gérard asked when we were sipping coffee in my somewhat austere office at the embassy.

"Well, you know, by rights it should be I, seeing that the reactor in question has been selected to be the Westinghouse Pressurized Water Reactor (PWR)," I responded. "However, in this mixed-up world things are not that simple. The United States Congress is dead set on denying the Chinese Communist regime the acquisition of a U. S. patented nuclear reactor from an American company. It will not happen. So, it is most likely that the French government will make this sale of a Westinghouse product. And you will get the credit. In fact, my boss, the commercial counselor has just obtained this book of specifications, which he received from a private contractor. He told me that I am free to give it to you, seeing that the U.S. Government forbids any sale to the Chinese by a U.S. agency. Here it is, and good luck!"

So, it happened: The French Nuclear Agency sold the Westinghouse PWR reactor and installed it on Chinese soil. This was the outstanding example of a high level enterprise that I was close to and it was really exciting for Gérard and me. It also demonstrated the lack of logic. The U.S. Congress did not allow a U.S. company to sell a nuclear reactor to a Communist country. The result was that the PRC bought it from France.

The second year at the U.S. Embassy in Beijing I was promoted to the diplomatic rank of Counselor, in charge of the newly created Section of Science and Technology with a secretary of my own. Also the newly-appointed ambassador, Arthur Hummel, arrived. Staff meetings of Counselors were held in a "secure area," meaning that it had been examined and cleared of any listening devices. In such a meeting one of the attendees spoke up:

"Otto is the only one here who does not know who I am. I am the Station Chief," meaning that he was the chief CIA officer at the embassy.

ROOTS LOST-ROOTS FOUND

I later was told that the station chief is known to the host government, and on a reciprocal basis, the station chief at the People's Republic of China (PRC) Embassy in Washington is known to the U.S. government. This arrangement sounds a bit strange but it is how it worked. It is as if the countries agreed to spy and to be spied upon.

One day I was asked to meet the ambassador in a secure area. When I arrived, the station chief was also present.

"We have decided to place a CIA agent 'undercover' in the Science Section," Ambassador Hummel said. "Her name is Ann. When she arrives it will be your job to pick her up at the airport. She will work on jobs you will assign to her on a half-time basis. You will be expected to take her along to meetings, and introduce her as your assistant. You will have to avoid revealing her undercover status and you will discuss anything relating to her and her activities only with me. Do you have any questions or objections to these arrangements?"

I felt put on the spot but saw no valid grounds for disagreement. Ann turned out to be a youngish and pleasant woman but she was not thorough when performing the tasks I assigned to her. I concluded that I had to check on her work. I hoped that she was more effective in her other work. In any case, I now had a section with a secretary and another staff member. And I could claim that I was the founding counselor at the Science Section of the embassy.

I usually went to work on Saturdays and on one such day I happened to cross the courtyard when I saw a Chinese man who seemed to drop into the embassy grounds over the top of the surrounding wall. I was taken aback and did not know what to do. He told me that he wanted to seek refuge. The best thing I thought of doing was to go to the station chief's office and, not finding him at his desk, I told a person there what I had witnessed. I then went to the DCM's office and, finding him at his desk I told him what I had seen. To my surprise, he told me that he had already asked the station chief's assistant to take over. I was glad to be relieved of responsibility for the incident and went back to my work. Some hours later I saw an embassy staff member take the Chinese intruder in a car to the embassy's entrance and deliver him to a police car waiting there. I never found out what happened, and no announcement came from any embassy source. It was one of those events shrouded in mystery and destined to remain obscure.

During my second year in Beijing, I received an invitation by telephone from the famous Chinese American physicist T.D. Lee to have lunch at the Beijing Hotel with him and his wife, specially prepared for them by the hotel chef. Everything in China arranged for TD was special. The invitation was transmitted to me by an official of the Chinese Academy of Sciences. There was no reason I was aware of for this invitation. Therefore, I concluded that Lee would ask me for a favor. Sure enough, he wanted *me* to write a letter of introduction for *him* to the U.S. consul in Shanghai. I assured him that he was so famous that he did not need a letter from me (poor little me) but I hurried to assure him that, nevertheless, I would do this immediately. It seemed that he wanted a favor from the Shanghai Consulate for a relative. So do the mighty sometimes stoop to ask a low-level acquaintance for a favor and in his perceived moment of need he remembered *me!* This was also a signal recognition for me and I will ask my daughters to inscribe on my gravestone in golden letters: IN 1981 THE MIGHTY TD LEE ASKED HIM FOR A LETTER OF INTRODUCTION!

Otto Schnepp

In July 1981 I left Beijing with Judith on the completion of my appointment and returned to Los Angeles and USC. Before leaving, Ambassador Hummel conferred on me in a small ceremony the SUPERIOR HONOR AWARD of the State Department, citing my contribution to the implementation of the U.S.-China Science and Technology Cooperation Agreement.

Chapter 18

Nepal Trek

The Himalaya exerts a magical attraction and fires up the imagination of most people — the mountain chain with the highest peaks on earth! The highest of the high — Mt. Everest — has been a challenge for mountain climbers since the first attempt to reach the summit in 1922.

The first question to be posed is: how did the Himalayas come into existence and how did it come about that its peaks are so high? It turns out that there are answers to these questions. Since the mid-1960s it has been accepted among geologists that the earth is composed of nine tectonic plates, which have moved relative to each other over time. 225 million years ago, Tibet and India, located on the Indian Plate, constituted a large island, situated off the Australian coast, separated from the Asian continent (part of the Eurasian Plate) by a large ocean, called the Tethys Sea. This island began moving northward about 200 million years ago, following the breakup of Pangaea, hypothesized as a super-continent that existed during the Paleozoic and Mesozoic eras about 250 million years ago, before the component continents were separated into their current configuration. About 80 million years ago India was located about 6,400 km (4,000 miles) south of the Asian continent, moving northward at the rate of 9 meters (or about 30 feet) per century. When In-dia, with Tibet on the northern edge of the Indian Plate, rammed into Asia about 40-50 million years ago, its northward advance was slowed by about half. Geologists interpret the collision and associated decrease in the rate of plate movement to mark the beginning of the rapid uplift of the Himalaya.

The two colliding plates are composed of rock of similar density (or hardness), which precluded one of these plates sliding over the other, forcing the buckling, and rise at the collision edge. The Hima-laya and the Tibetan Plateau to the north have risen relatively rapidly, causing the high peaks, such as Mt. Everest, to rise to heights of over 9 km (about 29,570 ft) over a period of just 50 million years. The impinging of the two landmasses is still continuing and the Himalayas continue to rise more than one centimeter a year, or one inch over 2 ½ years.

The challenge to climb Mt. Everest has attracted attempts since the first British expedition in 1922, following a reconnaissance expedition in 1921. But it took over thirty years until Edmund Hillary, a New Zealander, and Tenzing Norgay, a Nepalese Sherpa climber, reached the summit for the first time as part of the ninth British Mt. Everest expedition, on May 29th 1953. Previous attempts claimed a number of lives.

My first exposure to detailed information about Nepal came around 1970 when a friend — a former neighbor and leader of several hikes in Israel — told me about his visit to this country. Nick's unique characterization went something like this:

"I managed to get on a local airline flight within the country. This was a remarkable experience! When flying, I expect to look *down* onto mountains from the plane. But there, I had to look *up* at the mountain peaks — that is how high the Himalayan mountains are relative to, for example, the capital, Kathmandu, which lies at an altitude of 4,600 ft compared to many peaks' altitude of over 25,000 ft.

Standard cruising altitudes of planes are in the range of 10,000–30,000 ft.

Some years later, in 1970, I had an opportunity to experience Nepal myself when I visited there on my trip to Israel from Los Angeles by way of Japan. My first impression on landing was that I had gone through a time tunnel, like in the movies, and had arrived several centuries earlier. I hired a VW bug whose driver spoke a reasonably good and under-standable English. He told me that his car had been brought to Kathmandu in parts and was reassem-bled there. There were, at the time, no roads con-necting to cities outside Nepal. At that time I spent several hours at the airport of Pokhara, on the shores of a scenic lake. The day was particularly clear and I was fascinated by the view of the Annapurna moun-tain, which towers over the lake and whose summit is 8091 meters above sea level (26,400 ft). I shall re-turn to write more about Pokhara and the Annapur-na later on.

For several years I nurtured the idea of trekking in Nepal. This plan was attractive to me in several ways. I have always loved to hike and to be outside in nature, to explore and to sleep under the stars. Also it would be an adventure in a foreign country whose culture I did not know much about. It would be a challenge. As I read about trekking in Nepal, the idea came to me to investigate if I could share this adventure with my grandsons. The younger, Yuval, was going to have his Bar Mitsvah in August 1995, which means that he was approaching his 13th birthday. The older, Eran, was getting to be 16. They both lived in Haifa, Israel, where they were born and grew up — the sons of my older daughter, Debbie. I decided to broach the subject with her and her husband, Natti, short for Natan-El. They seemed to be supportive of my suggestion.

Yuval's Bar Mitsvah on July 30 gave me the opportunity to spend some time with his parents and to confirm the plan.

"How do you feel about my taking the boys on a trek to Nepal?" I asked them.

"We have discussed it and we think it is a good idea. This will also give you and the boys a great opportunity to spend time together and to share an adventure that they will remember for the rest of their lives. But we have wondered if you are up to this. After all, you are 70 years old!"

"I appreciate your concern for my safety but I am really confident that I will be fine. Yes, I have taken up doing a routine workout. As you know, I swim 30 laps regularly, and I have also been exercising on a walking machine, getting my pulse rate up above 100 per minute. My physician has also recently given me a stress test and I did very well. I will, of course, take out adequate travel insurance. Now let's discuss some details. We will fly from Tel Aviv to Athens by Olympic Airlines and from there we will continue by Thai Airlines to Bangkok and then on to Kathmandu, the capital of Nepal. There will be significant layovers in Athens and Bangkok. What do you suggest we do during these breaks?"

Debbie responded, "Athens is obvious. If you have the time, go and visit the Acropolis. The boys will be interested in exploring the temples and this will be a good educational experience as well."

Natti added, "The boys can read up on Greek history in addition to their reading a guide book for trekking in Nepal. Eran has already found appropriate books in Hebrew. It turns out that Nepal is a favorite for Israeli youngsters to visit after their army service."

Debbie added, "This all sounds good. Just waiting around at the airport would bore the boys and would make them cranky. I am also sure that Eran will read a lot in preparation for the trip. I am not so sure that Yuval will make the same level of effort."

I replied: "It doesn't much matter how much Yuval will work at preparing for the trip. I am pretty sure that he will catch up later, motivated by his memories.".

The first leg of the trip from Tel Aviv to Athens passed without problems, except that we had to leave the house in Haifa at 2:00 a.m. and I had to awaken the boys and oversee their getting ready. Debbie was also awake to supervise. We had packed the bags the day before. In addition to the usual suitcases, I had brought along a big duffle bag to pack our hiking boots and other outdoor clothing during the flight and to be carried along on the trek — hopefully by a hired porter.

On arrival in Athens we stored our carry-on bags and passed through Passport Control, I changed some money to local currency and we headed for the taxi stand. There I checked times of travel to the Acropolis to make sure that we would be able to return in time for the departure of our flight to Bangkok, and we were off. The tour of the Acropolis was a smashing success. The boys could not get enough of the ancient buildings, prepared as they were for viewing archaeological sites, which abound in Israel. Eran kept track of the dimensions, numbers of columns at the various temples, dates of building and the like. He was always, from an early age, a great one to gather statistics, which he somehow managed to store in his head and bring up in conversation later on. He also carried with him a guidebook he had brought from Israel and had studied estensively. Yuval, at this stage, was a loyal admirer of his older brother whom he followed around, asking him many questions.

"How high are these columns and how did they erect them without cranes, and who were the workers who did all this?"

Yuval piled on the questions in a continuous chain and did not allow time for answers. The few times that he did stop and Eran responded, he was already looking at something new that attracted his attention and clearly did not listen. I tried to contribute to the conversation to show my store of knowledge, but I was no match for Eran supported by his guidebook.

It was time to tear ourselves away from the ancient Greek archaeology and to return to the airport.

ROOTS LOST-ROOTS FOUND

There were lots of taxis waiting and we got into the first one in line. I communicated to the driver that we were in a hurry to go to the airport and he seemed to understand our situation. I did wonder about the man sitting in the passenger seat next to the driver but, not speaking Greek, there was no way I could get straight answers to my questions about him. We soon witnessed that the mysterious passenger got off some place but, to my dismay, we waited for his return. My anxiety increased by the minute and eventually the man returned and got back in. Then there was more anxiety since we clearly were cruising through city streets and there were no signs for the airport. I do have a small advantage in that I can read the Greek letters, which I had learned in the course of my studies of math and science and I was pretty sure I could recognize the Greek equivalent of the word "airport."

"I do hope we will get there in time!" I said to the boys for my own comfort but did not want them to tune in too much to my feelings and become overly anxious. I knew that Eran has always had some tendency to anxiety. Then, we made another stop and the man finally got out and stayed out. We were at last on our way to the airport as confirmed by the road signs. And my watch still continued ticking away the minutes as my heart beat out my apprehension in unison.

Finally, and to my great relief, the airport came within view and we had arrived. Then, another hurdle — a long line for checking in. Again the waiting and my anxiety returned. We were at the end of the line and I worried about overbooked flights. Would we get on? This time I decided not to share my fears with the boys. On the contrary, I reassured them that we were safe, as long as we were already in line. Time passed, as passengers checked their bags in and went off to Passport Control and the gate. Our progress was slow, all too slow! Finally, we were there and with pounding heart I presented our tickets and passports. The airline representative looked over our papers and finally spoke:

"You see, the cabin class is full." And my heart missed a beat. "Therefore, we had to advance you to business class," she completed her speech. Big breath of relief, and then some joy! *Business Class!* The words reverberated in my head. Our being late had paid off! I grabbed the papers and the boarding passes and stepped away. Then I took the boys to a bench, sat them down and I explained. They now shared my relief and joy.

"Mazal tov lanu!" (Hebrew equivalent of "cool"), Yuval shouted out.

And so we travelled more comfortably and more elegantly fed to Bangkok, a flight of 9½ hours.

On arrival in Bangkok, I found an airline representative who directed me to a short-time rooming facility and we trotted off. One minor difficulty — they took only cash — no credit cards. However, they accepted U.S. currency! Okay! I paid and we checked into a "day room" which was adequate for two persons and tight for three. Eran and Yuval stretched out on the queen-size bed crosswise to leave some room for me and promptly fell asleep. I was more ambitious, undressed, brushed my teeth, shaved and took a shower before lying down. This time there was no crisis and no taxi problem; we were there in time for the next leg of our journey to Kathmandu. But also there was no upgrade — we went cabin class for the 2½ hour flight.

Arriving in Kathmandu we faced a long line for Passport Control but there were no significant delays and we cleared through in reasonable time.

"Now we have to find our luggage," I announced. "Yuval, you guard our carry-on bags, and Eran and I will go and search."

The bags were just standing around in a big hangar-like room and there was no real method for locating ours. We found two out of three bags quickly, but the third, the duffle bag, so essential for our adventure, was nowhere. I saw a large pile of bags under the control of an American (by his speech) and I told him what we were looking for.

"No use looking here," he told me with a tone of great assurance. "This is all baggage of Peace Corps members."

We continued our search — after delivering the two recovered bags to Yuval. Nothing. Then I found a friendly airline rep and he was sympathetic and urged me to begin filling out forms to report lost baggage. I was in mourning. My head was swirling with thoughts of what we needed to buy to continue on our venture. I felt a bitter taste of despair slowly rising inside me. Then — out of the blue — Eran appeared holding the lost duffle bag.

"Eifo matsata oto? Where did you find it?" I shot out.

"I was not put off by the American guarding the Peace Corps baggage! *Ve sham zeh haya!* And there it was under a pile of other duffle bags!" was Eran's explanation — plain and simple.

I was furious. A large part of my anger was at myself, a world-seasoned traveler, being shown up and outdone by my 16-year-old grandson! I went to give this American a piece of my mind and accused him of all sorts of criminal acts. But then — what was most important was that we had recovered the bag, and so I eventually let go of my anger, turned my back on the culprit after a final volley of curses and we walked off. I found the hotel reservation service and rented a room at the "Yellow Pagoda." We set off by taxi, and immediately after arrival, I went to a nearby travel agent to make arrangements for transportation to Pokhara, our jumping-off point for the trek the next morning.

"I can get you the papers you need — the trekking permits — delivered to your hotel at 4 p.m. But, there are no seats by plane available for tomorrow to Pokhara. I can offer you two choices. A private car costs $200. Or you can go by tourist bus for $5 per person," the agent told me.

Otto Schnepp

Well, I thought, $15 compared to $200 sounds like a good deal, even if it may take a little longer. Little did I know what awaited us on the bus trip! The bus was scheduled to leave at 7 a.m. and would arrive in Pokhara at about 2 p.m., I was told. Not so bad for a distance of 200 km (or 124 miles). The guidebook description of the trip, however, sounded a warning. "Road conditions are appalling for the first 100 km, so it takes eight to nine hours for the 200 km trip."

I obstinately held to my optimistic outlook and decided to proceed with the bus option.

We were there for the scheduled departure of the "tourist bus," but it took another 20 minutes to get everybody on board and get going. The three of us did not sit together and this turned out to be a good choice. In my notes I wrote: "The road was terrible — ghastly." As I recall, there was a steep descent near the beginning and the road was not only full of potholes but it looked like a scene after a strong earthquake. There really was not much of a road at all, just random pieces of pavement scattered over an uneven earthen roadbed. There also were many vehicles of all descriptions, like I had seen in movies on location in India. In fact, it turned out that this was a major road to India. After about three hours, the road improved and our progress was faster. I was relieved and felt more relaxed.

At about 11 a.m. we had a tire blow out — a sharp crack followed by a somewhat bumpy ride. The bus stopped and we all got off to watch the proceedings. The right rear was a double tire, perhaps a double wheel, and the inner tire was flat. The driver decided to change a spare for the damaged tire. I learned that there was an assistant on the bus who did the work under the supervision of the driver. The operation took about thirty minutes and we were off again. At noon we stopped for lunch. Of the available choices, I picked the least risky looking ones — crackers, a choice of "MALT" and "COCO-NUT." There also was a sweet, called "TWIX," and there were bottled drinks.

An hour later, about 1 p.m., the traffic stopped. Our bus was fourth in line before a barrier. My neighbor, a Nepali, translated an announcement by the driver: "There was a truck that went off the road seven days before."

I saw the truck lying on its side by the road. We had to wait and watch an attempt to haul the truck onto the road in order to have it towed away. There was no crane — just a big truck with a rope. The attempt failed and the road was cleared to allow the traffic to move on.

A loud explosion shook the bus at about 2:30 p.m., originating from the back of the bus. The driver decided that another bus had been the cause and he continued. This went all right for another ten minutes until we passed through a town, and there our trip suddenly turned bumpy. It had been our bus, after all! We got off again and could look at what happened. The spare that they had mounted (to replace the blown tire) had cracked wide open with the inner tube clearly visible. This time they decided to have the original punctured tire repaired and mount it in place of the spare.

This operation took a while, and we had time to get acquainted with our fellow passengers. The bus had 27 seats, of which 20 were occupied by tourists, and eight turned out to be Israelis. The boys made friends with all eight, exchanged information about who they were, where they lived in Israel and what their plans were. I chatted with two women who were government workers from Guam. There also were two young Nepali men — one seemed smart, had good English and told me that he was studying in a Jesuit school in Kathmandu. The other one was working for the travel company that owned the bus! In fact, he had issued our tickets! They agreed that Kathmandu had changed a great deal during the twenty years since I had been there the first time. We had not had time to see the city yet on this trip and I looked forward to taking a look on our return. We continued our bus journey after about an hour.

We arrived at 5:30 p.m. at the Pokhara bus station. It had not been the smooth ride I had expected, and I felt that we had learned a lot about transportation in Nepal. If we had succeeded in getting tickets to fly to Pokhara from Kathmandu, this would have taken just 30 minutes, but then we would have missed all the adventure and the people we met.

It was already getting dark. We were received by a number of locals offering taxi services and hotel reservations. We took a taxi to the hotel for which we had prepaid in Kathmandu, called Tibet Resort. Our room had three beds and a spacious bathroom equipped with a shower without a curtain. I was able to make arrangements for our return from the end point of our trek at Jomsom back to Pokhara by air and for a continuing flight to Katmandu. I also arranged for a taxi to take us to the start-up point of our trek the next morning and for a porter to accompany us for the ten days we would be out of contact with the world. The next morning we awoke to the sounds of thunder and rain.

It was September 29 and this was the day we began our trek for real. We left the hotel at 5:30 in the morning without having breakfast. The rain had stopped and our taxi was waiting. We went to pick up the porter on the way. He turned out to be a short, stocky and pleasantly smiling chap. His name was Korká. I would guess that he was about 25 to 30. I had good vibes from him, but Eran's face bore a grim expression.

"*Ma yesh, Eran?* What is the matter, Eran?" I asked him.

He just grunted, in response. I decided not to question him further. I believe that he felt anxiety in response to the unfamiliar surroundings and people at close quarters. I was confident that he would get acclimatized after getting out into the open country.

We rode in the taxi for about an hour, to a point just below a village called Birethanti at an elevation of 1065 m and we walked for about twenty minutes to reach the village, where we had breakfast, bought a basket for Korká, and a walking stick for Yuval. I was going to buy one for myself when a youngish

German couple saw us at the restaurant, and the woman offered me her stick since they had just ended their trek "around Annapurna" which was a bit more ambitious than our plans. I accepted gratefully and we were all equipped. Eran decided that he did not need a stick. The baskets for porters are furnished with a broad band which lies on the forehead, usually protected by a hat made of woven material, the near-conically-shaped basket lying on the back of the porter. This is not a configuration we are used to and I had never before encountered it. The load is supported by the forehead, not the shoulders, as we do it.

We had lunch at Hille, after climbing up about 400 m or 1,300 ft. After lunch we continued upwards and soon after leaving Hille, the trail took the form of a stone staircase all the way up to Ulleri at 2070 m or 6,800 ft for a difference of close to 610 m (2,000 ft). As we ascended this staircase, we stopped and rested at intervals. Soon, Yuval piped up.

"*Yesh li ke'ev rosh!* I have a headache," Yuval blurted out in a plaintive voice. I was at a loss as to how to react but Korká knew what to do, even though he could not communicate with us verbally. He relieved Yuval of his backpack and dumped it in his basket. Yuval quickly felt better and recovered. He must have reacted to the rapid change in altitude and the weight of his backpack made a difference.

As we progressed slowly up the stairs, two large mountains came into view — Annapurna South (7,273 m) and Hinchuli (6336 m), all covered with snow, offering a spectacular view and giving us great encouragement in our climb. Arriving at Ulleri and feeling that we had earned a good rest, we settled in a hotel suggested by Korká. It turned out that other trekkers had already stopped there. We met again four Swedish young women with whom I had chatted at our lunch stop. They had a Nepali guide who was a cut above our porter and he spoke English quite well. This turned out to be really useful since he could orient us and also helped us communicate with Korká.

"Why can you not talk with Korká?" Yuval asked out of the blue. "You speak Chinese, don't you?"

"Yes, I know some Chinese but here they speak a language called Nepali. I don't know that. It is quite different from Chinese. Also, I cannot read Nepali; it is written using an alphabet that is similar to Sanskrit. This is the original language on which many European languages are based. I understand that also the Semitic languages are related to it. For example, the word *air* is derived from Sanskrit, I have been told. That is why it is common to many languages, including Ivrit (Hebrew) in which it is *avir*, as you know. This is clearly related to the English word 'air.'"

"*Zeh me'anyane me'od!* This is very interesting!" Yuval and Eran said, almost in unison.

So my grandsons had assumed I could talk to people in Nepal on the basis of their knowing that I speak Chinese. I had to set them straight and disavow them of that assumption. The world is more complex and multilingual than they had thought. At this opportunity I also was able to show off some other scraps of information I had picked up here and there.

We settled into two rooms, each containing two simple wooden cots with a gap between the partition separating the rooms and the ceiling, large enough to allow easy communication between the rooms. This inn was run by a brother and sister team. It was cloudy and it rained before darkness fell and therefore we could not see the view. But at about 9 p.m. our host alerted us that the weather had cleared and he pointed out the mountains visible in the moonlight, which were the same we had seen during our climb up the rock staircase. However, we could never get enough sightings of these magnificent giants. I also took a shower, which felt wonderful. The hot water in many of these lodges was supplied with the aid of solar heating. Only rarely was there a connection to generator-supplied electricity.

I also did a bit of laundry. On the trek, the laundry is done at night and hung up to dry overnight. Usually, it is not quite dry by morning and then the articles of underwear, which is the usual category of laundry, are attached to the outside of the backpack with safety pins until quite dry. I had been prepared for the ways of the trek from my readings of the guidebook that I had bought in Los Angeles.

We had brought water for the first day in bottles that we had filled at the hotel in Pokhara. But from now on, each morning we would have to prepare our water for the day before setting out, by purifying the continuously flowing water as supplied from plastic pipes outside these primitive inns and passing it through filters I had bought from the REI store. The water comes down the hillside from wells uphill. It was necessary to filter the water because its path was of an uncertain level of cleanliness. We also brought sleeping bags to serve as bedding, which during the trekking were stowed in the duffle bag carried by Korká in his basket. This basket seemed to have an almost unlimited capacity, and he was able to carry it all.

The food was a staple called *dhal baat*, a mixture of cooked lentils and rice with various special additions that varied from place to place. The latter usually consisted of mashed potatoes flavored with vegetables and spices. It seemed that each village had its own special side dish. We drank our water, and tea was served at all of the inns. In some places there was freshly squeezed apple juice. Occasionally there also was apple pie, but this was the exception.

The daily routine was to set out early, by about 8 in the morning and to walk until about 4 p.m. with an hour for lunch. On some rare occasions we continued until 5 or even 6 p.m., but then we encountered some difficulties finding adequate accommodations. Once we only could get one room with two cots and we had to push them together for all three of us to have something to sleep on.

"I want to lie in the middle between Saba (Grandpa) and Yuval," Eran said with some intensity. "I would not be able to sleep on the outside. I am afraid of falling off!" Eran concluded.

We complied with Eran's request and it all ended well.

Usually, we climbed about 500-600 meters in the course of a day and there were also drops by similar heights. The trail was comfortable most of the time, but in some places it was washed out, and I was grateful for the support of my walking stick when there were such spots, since the trail led across steep slopes. Eran managed well throughout without a stick.

The views of the high snow-covered mountains were great and often spectacular. We also crossed some fields covered with wonderfully colored flowers, and forests, e.g. the magnificent oak and rhododendron forests (so described in the guidebook) above Ulleri on the trail to Ghorapani. The trail again passes through rhododendron and magnolia forests beyond Ghorapani on the way to Tatopani. This last name means hot water and indeed this village is special in that it is the site of a hot spring which is mixed with cold water from the Gandaki River to feed a very pleasantly hot pool where trekkers congregate to heal their stressed muscles. This memorable spot is deeply carved into my memory. I remember also seeing our Swedish friends again there in the pool.

On the trail, we often encountered fast-moving mule trains and had to duck into the bushes on the side of the trail to avoid being trampled. The pack animals range from large mules to small burros, no bigger than large dogs. The lead animals' heads are colorfully festooned and make for good photo opportunities. These mule trains are an important means of transporting cargo between Pokhara and Jomsom. The animals also carry pleasantly tinkling bells whose sounds carry far across the mountains and valleys along their route. It is remarkable how fast they move and it is even more remarkable that their tenders, Tibetan men, can keep up with them.

Police checkposts are fixtures along the trail. We checked in at one of these located at a pass called Deurali (Nepali for "pass") just beyond Ghorapani, (meaning horse water), elevation 2834 m. The police officer was a tall and powerfully built man, contrasting with the local village population, which is mostly short. He wanted to see our trekking permit and entered our personal details in an impressive-looking ledger. He also inscribed an endorsement on the permit which was proof that we had checked in with the police, as is required.

On arrival at Ghorapani we found accommodations, had some dinner and went to bed early after setting our alarms to wake us up at 4:30 a.m. Noisy neighbors woke us up before the alarms went off. We quickly dressed and left at 5 a.m. for an ascent of 300 m to reach Poon Hill, about an hour's climb, before sunrise. This hilltop is famous and the views were truly overpowering! White mountain peaks everywhere. Annapurna, Annapurna South, Hiunchuli, Machapuchara (fishtail). I took many photos and in my blind enthusiasm got a lot of duplicates. We constantly exclaimed in admiration and wonder and so did the other gathered trekkers.

"Look, here is Hiunchuli and there is Machapuchara. The fishtail shape is very clear from here! What a magnificent sight. I cannot get enough of these exciting views!"

The literal high point of our trek was the temple at Muktinat, at 3,800 m (12,500 ft), a pilgrimage site reputedly visited by a wide range of religious Hindus, from well-dressed women wearing jewelry to half-naked holy men (*sadhus*). We began our climb at Kagbeni, at 2,810 m, reputed to look like a town out of the medieval past whose inhabitants dress in typical Tibetan clothing. Because of the large difference in altitude to Muktinat (1,000 m or 3,000 ft), I took advantage of an opportunity to arrange for a horse for Yuval, and the man who led the horse also served as an additional porter to carry our backpacks, which relieved Korka's load on the steep climb. It was indeed a difficult climb and I had to stop a number of times to rest and also to catch my breath in the thin mountain air. We started out at 7:00 a.m. and arrived at the hotel in Mukhtinat at a little after noon. Rental of the horse cost $10 and the additional porter cost $4. Yuval enjoyed the ride, although he said that he felt a bit uneasy looking down the steep slopes by the road from the added height of the horseback. At one point the horse waited for me to catch up, which I finally did and then I stopped to rest, out of breath.

After about two minutes, Yuval said from his perch on the horse: "*Sabba, nelech kvar!*" Or "Grandpa, let's go already!" This pronouncement provided fertile material for teasing Yuval for some time.

After a rest at the hotel, named the Mona Lisa Hotel, we went up a bit further to the temple and met the monk. He showed us some of the temples of the complex — for Krishna and Shiva. I made a small contribution and the monk put a red spot on my forehead, mumbling some prayer. Yuval also got one, but Eran declined the honor. A second monk appeared, perhaps a Buddhist, and he repeated the same ceremony. We returned to the hotel, fighting our way through the aggressive and unrelenting group of hawkers, said to be Tibetans and offering woolen scarves, wraps and souvenirs. I bought two pieces of *saligram*, which are black stones that when cracked open, reveal fossilized remains of prehistoric ammonites (marine snail-like animals), formed about 130 million years ago. These are unique to this region. Pilgrims buy them because they are reminders of the myths surrounding the Hindu god Vishnu. Yuval selected two ammonites, one for Eran and himself and one for me to keep.

Back at the hotel it was cozy. There was a large table with a blanket draped around it and glowing embers in a dish under it. It was good and warm to sit there with my legs under the blanket, eating warm apple pie and sipping apple cider. I met several other foreign trekkers: two Scots, and one Australian among them. They were taking the trek "around Annapurna" and had that day crossed the

Thorung Pass at 5,416 m (almost 18,000 ft). They told of their experiences, particularly how each of them handled the high altitude. Some did well and others spent a sleepless night, gasping for air. I could not match their stories, except that they had not yet been to Poon Hill. I had enough problems with the altitude of Muktinat.

That night I slept only fitfully. When lying on my side, as I usually do, I woke up, feeling anxious and gasping for air. Then, turning to lie flat on my back, with regular breathing, I calmed down and recovered. I eventually fell asleep but soon woke up again, lying on my side and again gasping for air. This cycle repeated itself a number of times and I did not get much rest. The night did eventually pass and dawn came at about 5:30 a.m. The sky was cloudless and the view of Dhaulagiri from our window was, again, fantastic.

Breakfast was simple oatmeal — they say it comes in packages, I assume dehydrated, as it is also available at home. We began our descent on our way to Jomsom while admiring the grand vistas of snow-covered mountains. This was a lot easier and faster than climbing up to Muktinat. We kept on exchanging our feelings of delight and wonder at the views

— always similar, but we never could get enough of them. We arrived back in the valley of the Kali Gandaki at about 10:30 a.m. This is, by the way, said to be the deepest gorge on earth, running between Annapurna I and the Dhaulagiri I mountains, both over 8,000 m with the low point at below 2,200 m, and the distance between the mountain peaks is only 38 km (23.5 miles).

Eran came up with the sobering fact that the highest altitude we had reached, 4,000 m, was still 500 m short of half the height of Everest! Not so impressive, when compared with the highest point on earth.

While traversing this gorge, winds become a problem after 11:00 a.m. Earlier, the wind is gentle but after that the wind is reputed to turn and howls up the gorge, kicking up dust and sand. This is exactly what we encountered. Also the vegetation changed radically as we progressed toward Jomsom, our exit airport, from pine and conifer forests to dry and sandy desert. It was like a sandstorm scene in the movies. At one point Eran and Korká were ahead and Yuval was falling behind. I decided that I had to wait for him and resolved to keep him within sight. The result was that we both fell behind and lost sight of Eran and Korká. I became anxious about being able to know which way the trail went in this barren landscape, with the cold wind blowing in our faces, but we just continued struggling along. It turned out that I had guessed correctly to continue straight and found Korká waiting for us. I was sure relieved to see him.

We traversed the whole town to check in at the Mona Lisa Hotel, near the airport. There was that name again. We now had two days to wait for our reserved flight back to Pokhara. I needed a good rest and enjoyed the lazy pace. The time was taken up taking photos of each of us against the backdrop of the Nelgiri mountain, in back of the hotel, updating our journals and taking walks in the town. I also had to settle accounts with Korká — a complicated calculation using a rate of Rs350 ($7) per day with a 10% tip and half the rate for his return to Pokhara with added allowance for food for a total of Rs5,000 ($100). I also gave him a present — an old down jacket of good quality but it had two small holes. I also offered him an old sweater, which he eagerly accepted. We parted on the best of terms. He seemed to be happy with his pay and presents.

Otto Schnepp

The next day, October 8, I slept well until I woke up at 3 a.m. gasping for air. The altitude in Jomsom is only 2,713 m or 8,950 ft, and I was surprised at my reaction. I rested after recovering. Then, at 4 a.m. there was a knock at my door. It was Eran, explaining that he had locked himself out. He forgot to take the key when he had an urgent call for the toilet — the second time that night. He lay down on the spare cot in my room. That morning I tried to persuade Yuval to take a shower and finally succeeded. Hurrah! The facilities were very good — there was hot water all day. After lunch we went for a walk to orient ourselves. The check-in counter of the primitive airport was just five minutes' walk from the hotel. Eran felt weak; he only had toast and tea for breakfast and lunch. His stomach was still turbulent. In the evening I prepared for packing and leaving early the next morning. I cleaned my boots, including the soles, and also cleaned Eran's since he was not well. I tried to urge Yuval to clean his boots. He protested and Eran supported him. They claimed that they had never heard of cleaning the soles of boots. I insisted and received some half-hearted responses. I guess they just wrote me off as some hopeless old man. Eventually we got things sorted out and packed. We prepared our water for the next day, had dinner and drank our last freshly squeezed apple juice. Then I paid our bill to be ready to depart early in the morning.

Again I spent a difficult night; I woke up several times. I slept for one to two hours and woke up gasping for air. We got up at 5 a.m., washed, brushed teeth and left, carrying our backpacks and I carried the duffle bag, which was not heavy. When we arrived at the gate promptly for the scheduled check in at 6:10 a.m. we found it locked. Soon agents of three airlines arrived and opened up. They slowly began checking in, we got our boarding passes and felt relieved. Next we waited for the planes to arrive. After an hour or so a siren sounded, and ten minutes later there was another blast of a siren. A small propeller plane landed — causing a stir of excitement among the waiting crowd of about 50-100. It was an Everest Airline plane, it was announced. After the arriving passengers disembarked, the departing passengers got on. The plane immediately took off. I saw the plane in the distance disappearing between the hills. Again, we waited. Tension was in the air. Everyone knew the local conditions: all departing planes must leave by 10:00 a.m. because of the rising winds after that. Finally, another siren: a large Nepal Airlines helicopter landed. Next there was another propeller plane from Everest Airlines. Both planes loaded up. Then, as the Everest Airlines plane was ready to take off, it stopped to allow another plane to land. This was a Royal Nepali Airline plane — ours! I breathed a sigh of relief. We boarded quickly and now all three waiting planes took turns taking off. We were in the air at last. The plane flew between Dhaulagiri Mountain on the right and the Annapurna Massif peaks on the left, giving us an amazing view. Many more peaks were visible, all towering above the plane. We landed at the Pokhara airport in short order, where we were greeted by a clear sky and another view of the many mountains visible there. I took some photos and we took a taxi to return to the Tibet Resort Hotel where we had left our baggage and had made a reservation before starting on our trek. Eran had recovered from his digestive disorder.

We returned to Kathmandu the next day, this time by plane. I went into town to look around, but neither Eran nor Yuval could be persuaded to come along. I was disappointed that they were not curious to see the city. But then, they evidently had had enough of strange and perhaps threatening environments. Next, we flew back to Bangkok for a day of sightseeing, a night at a hotel and then on to Tel Aviv by way of Athens, retracing our outbound route.

I was glad that we had made it back with everybody in good physical shape and we had brought back with us a great deal of memories to chew over. Predictably, the shared experience has been a strong bond between the boys and myself and we never get tired of reminiscing.

Chapter 19

Arieh and the Nobel Prize

The ringing of the telephone awoke me — I was still half-dozing as I picked up. I recognized the voice of my younger daughter, Tamar, through a thick fog of drowsiness.

"Dad, wake up, I just heard on the radio — Arieh Warshel got the Nobel Prize!"

All I could do was to utter with incredulity, "What?"

And then I was wide awake. "Really? Wow — that's wonderful!"

"Yes, really! I was in the shower and had the radio on. And then I heard the news that the Nobel Committee has just announced the winners of the Nobel Prize in Chemistry for 2013. There are three winners, and Arieh Warshel is one of them! As soon as I got out of the shower, I called you."

"But how did you recognize his name? How come you remembered it?"

"You have talked a lot about him and so I have heard his name mentioned often. Also, I remember that he was at our house at least once," Tamar responded.

The news stimulated a flood of memories: I have known Arieh since 1968. I met him when I visited Israel and Shneior Lifson, who was a professor at the Weizmann Institute in Rehovot, hosted me. Arieh was his Ph.D. student. We co-authored and published a paper. But this was so long ago that I hardly remember what it was about. I must ask Arieh — I am sure he will remember. I invited him to visit USC when he was looking for a permanent job. The faculty liked his seminar, although after the seminar he said he was worried about not wearing a tie during his presentation. I assured him that I participated in many faculty meetings discussing candidates and never heard a tie mentioned. At any rate, we recruited him and he has been at USC ever since 1976.

That day, Wednesday, October 9, 2013, I tried to phone Arieh at his office, and instead I got a secretary in the departmental office. She recognized my voice.

"Dr. Schnepp, I know why you are calling. Dr. Warshel is very busy answering calls from newspaper and television journalists."

"I will tell you what. Please take a message: I send him my congratulations," I responded. And that was it. Overnight, literally, Arieh had become a worldwide celebrity and could not be easily reached any more. What an amazing change!

On the following Monday morning, I thought I would try again. I dialed Arieh's office number and, behold, I heard his voice with his thick Hebrew-Israeli accent, saying: "Alo."

"Arieh, you answer your telephone yourself! What a pleasant surprise. I tried to call you and congratulate you last Wednesday but without success! Did you get my message?"

"To tell the truth, I don't know. I had so many messages that day, I couldn't keep track. Today is the first day that I have come to the office. I have been besieged at home and could not get out before."

"You are right, of course. That was a silly question. So, when do you go to Sweden to collect your prize?" I inquired.

Arieh's response surprised me:*"Aineni yode'a. Av-al kodem ar'eh et yedidha badereh.* (I don't know but first, on the way I will see your friend)."

"Who is that friend of mine whom you have time to visit?" I asked.

"Obama," was his short reply.

"Oh, so you have been invited to visit the White House!" I exclaimed.

"Yes, I will go there on the way to Stockholm. But even before that, I will see Putin in Kazakhstan. You know, this used to be Russia."

"Now you are really traveling! No, you are in global orbit," I responded. "And how is Tammi? How is she dealing with all that's going on?"

"She cannot sleep at night. She worries about what to wear for all these occasions! And my grand-daughter has been elected president of her class in elementary school on the strength of my prize. By the way, I have referred some reporters to you for more information about me and how I got to USC."

"Well, thank you very much for elevating me to the level of being newsworthy. But now, Arieh, you must stop...."

Arieh interrupted me: "stop fighting people, this I cannot promise!"

I chuckled and responded: "No Arieh, I meant to say that you have to stop complaining that you are not recognized by the scientific community."

"This, I think, I will be able to do, but only after a while," he answered.

"I am glad that I had this opportunity to talk to you. I imagine that it will be more difficult in the near term until things calm down again. Once more I wish you *mazal tov* (congratulations and good luck) and I also wish you *harbei oneg venahat* (much joy and satisfaction)."

I felt the need to discuss Arieh's prize some more, and I next phoned an old friend and colleague at USC — David.

"Well, what do you say about Arieh's Nobel Prize?" I began.

"I am thrilled. Really, more than pleased. We both know that he fought hard with the reviewers of the publications and with the editors of the journals."

I responded: "Yes, he fought with everybody. I often had lunch with Arieh and he always had stories about how the reviewers cast doubts on his results and how his submitted papers were rejected. But, slowly he gained recognition and was invited to present papers at prestigious conferences. Was it necessary for him to fight that hard? Not everybody does that. After he was elected to the National Academy of Sciences (NAS) a few years ago, he calmed down some. I saw him at a symposium in March and had lunch with him, just he and I — although he was very much in demand. We spoke Hebrew, which discouraged others from interrupting. I asked him then if and how his life had changed with his election. He told me that there was one big change — he no longer needed to fight with reviewers. He would get preferential treatment by the *Proceedings of the NAS* which is a prestigious publication."

I next called Ranty, a former student of mine. I reached him at his number at JPL (Jet Propulsion Laboratories) in Pasadena, which I had in my iPhone directory.

"Hi, Ranty. What do you say about Arieh being awarded the Nobel Prize?"

He responded: "I have been telling everybody around here that now it turns out that I had a future Nobel Laureate on my thesis committee!"

"More than that," I remarked, "you are a co-author of a Nobel prize winner on the publication based on your thesis, Arieh contributed to the interpretation of your experimental results."

The next day I received phone calls from two writers for USC publications. One of them told me that Arieh mentioned me several times while she interviewed him and told her that I had made it possible for him to succeed in his academic work. I assured her that this was a gross exaggeration, but it is true that I had something to do with getting him to USC. I added that we have two joint publications, but neither was in the field for which he was cited in the Nobel Prize announcement. We talked a lot about Arieh's difficulties having his work recognized by the theoretical chemistry establishment. The reporter asked me on what I had based my judgment that he was of interest to the chemistry department. I told her that I had recognized that he had a deep understanding of the science and that he seemed energetic and motivated. I arranged for him to be invited to visit and give a seminar — all being part of the regular procedure for a faculty prospect. Arieh impressed the faculty of the department, and we decided to recruit him.

Now let's go back to Arieh's difficulty to be recognized. He addressed complex problems that had not been tackled before. The established leaders in the field of theoretical chemistry judged his aims to be too ambitious and beyond probable success. They wanted to stay within certain boundaries and to pursue research projects dealing with simpler molecules. Arieh wanted to go beyond the established boundaries. His co-awardee of the Nobel Prize, Martin Karplus, advised interviewers that leaders in theoretical chemistry told him that he was wasting his time. The direct quote is:

"My chemistry colleagues thought it was a waste of time." He added "…the next generation of scientists should be courageous and not necessarily believe their colleagues if they say that something cannot be done."

The Nobel committee listed the Scientific Background for the Nobel Prize as:

"DEVELOPMENT OF MULTISCALE MODELS FOR COMPLEX CHEMICAL SYSTEMS."

Arieh told a reporter from the Reuters news agency that he had been convinced of the case for using computers to simulate chemical reactions involving *enzymes* ever since 1975, but did not know if he would live to see that accepted by the scientific community.

"I always knew that it was the right direction," he said, "but I had infinite difficulties and setbacks in the research. None of my papers were ever published without being rejected first, based on reviewers' criticism." This is the fate of a real innovator. The "establishment" in the profession resists change until compelled to accept it.

In reviewing his scientific career, Arieh himself has written that he was motivated from an early time by curiosity — how does something work? In particular, he wanted to understand how enzymes work.

What are enzymes and what do they do? We can say that enzymes are *catalysts* in all chemical reactions in the body, including reactions causing the decomposition and digestion of food in the body, as well as reactions resulting in the conversion of small molecules from one form to another to build molecules that are crucial for life. To cite another example, enzymes break up a long chain of sugar molecules into smaller parts. Proteins and enzymes are complex chemical systems, which means that they are composed of large molecules, each containing several thousand atoms. It is a great challenge to simulate by computer the way enzymes control and accelerate these chemical reactions. This is what these Nobel Prize awardees have achieved.

I am reminded of a conversation I had many years ago with a visitor from UC San Diego — Martin. After talking to Arieh he said of him:

"… This guy is afraid of nothing. He is willing to tackle very difficult, if not impossible problems. He might come up with something."

Well, it looks like he has.

Linus Pauling, Nobel Prize winner for the structure of proteins, and Watson and Crick (James D. Watson and Francis Crick), Nobel Prize winners for the structure of DNA, all used models looking superficially like pre-school children's toys constructed from plastic balls and sticks. These scientists relied on known chemical structural rules, derived from many years of experience. This type of modeling belongs to the past. The awardees of the 2013 Nobel Prize used computers to construct their models. They used complex mathematical methods to determine structures by seeking configurations of minimum potential energies. They benefitted from the great advances in available computer power, which could accommodate ever larger problems.

ROOTS LOST-ROOTS FOUND

Arieh is a person of medium stature, and he comes across as having a modest self-image. He does not project a commanding or leadership personality. He is even sometimes self-deprecating. He can make a strong statement, but then follows that up with the remark: "maybe not." This is a habit that is misleading and causes people to think that he is not sure of what he believes. Actually, he does have strong opinions and will fight hard to get them accepted. All this may have contributed to his difficulty in getting himself and his work accepted by his peer community. Some even still find it hard to accept him as brilliant, which he certainly is, and now he has been certified as such. Arieh turned out to be a successful teacher, in spite of his not being a native English speaker. The students liked him; he had a good sense of humor and prepared conscientiously for his classes.

The Royal Swedish Academy of Sciences, in a statement following the announcement of the 2013 prize, commented that the awardees "had effectively taken chemistry into cyberspace." Further, "the computer is (now) just as important a tool for chemists as the test tube." Also, ". . . powerful computer models, first developed by the three scientists (Arieh

Warshel, Michael Levi and Martin Karplus) in the 1970s, offer a new window into such reactions (between complex chemical systems) and have become a mainstay for researchers in thousands of academic and industrial laboratories around the world." And again "In drug design, for example, scientists can now use computers to calculate how an experimental medicine will react with a particular target protein in the body by working out the interplay of atoms."

The wide applications of the computational modeling methods testify to their usefulness in a great variety of fields and to their acceptance by the world scientific community.

Some days after the announcement of the prize, I tried again to contact Arieh, but I could only get to the departmental secretary, Michele, and I asked her to convey to him my message that I wanted to talk to him concerning what to tell the writers of USC publications whom he had referred to me. In response, Arieh asked Michele to send me a recent publication in which he outlined the history of his relevant scientific accomplishments and he also sent me an email message:

"Dear Otto, Sorry for not responding. I am completely overwhelmed by different interviews, emails, phone calls, events and much more. I will try to call if things calm down."

I did want an answer from him to one question in particular and decided to send him an email message in Hebrew, which I can do from my iPad. I thought that this would work. Not many people would be able to read it, which satisfied one concern of mine, and I thought that he would give preference to a message in Hebrew. Sure enough, I received his response the next morning.

I discovered that the announcement of the prize on October 9, 2013 can be seen as a video on the website of the Swedish Academy of Sciences. After the announcement in Swedish and its translation into English, the General Secretary of the Academy congratulated Arieh by phone and asked him how he felt. His response was:

"I feel very well now. I was a bit sleepy at first after answering your telephone call."

Another interviewer next asked him: "What were you doing when you received the call?" His response was to the point:

Otto Schnepp

"I was sleeping. This is usually what we do around here at 2 o'clock in the morning!"

I was more recently, over a year after the Nobel Prize announcement, interested to find out how Arieh's life has been affected since he received the prize and asked to make an appointment for a visit. From the dates he offered me, I chose Monday, February 16, which turned out to be Presidents' Day, and USC was closed. The disadvantage was that restaurant facilities on campus were not available and Arieh's new secretary had to arrange for lunch off-campus. However, the advantage was that there was almost nobody around and we were undisturbed. Only a few postdoctoral students were at work.

I easily found Arieh in his office, which had not been moved, but had undergone a major remodeling to make it more appropriate for his new stature. Walls were broken down and it now consisted of a tastefully arranged set of areas with display cases. These contained a number of certificates crowned by the Nobel Prize award certificate and diplomas certifying the honorary doctorates he had recently received.

Arieh told me that the greatest change in his financial affairs had been the establishment of a nonprofit foundation and some of his income was being deposited into this foundation. His share of the Nobel Prize was $460,000. It is likely that his salary from the university had about doubled since the announcement of the prize, but I assume that he also received a major increase after he was elected to the National Academy a few years ago. I estimate that his yearly university salary was now somewhere between $300,000 and $400,000. In addition he had an income stream from his invited lectures and invited participation in symposia worldwide. He remarked that he did a lot of travelling and was out of the country most of January of that year (2015). He visited Uppsala University in Uppsala, Sweden, where he received an honorary doctorate. He also visited Singapore where he received a Certificate of Gratitude for his contribution to the university's advancement in science.

Arieh is now the holder of an endowed chair — the Dana and David Dornsife Chair in Chemistry. The Dornsifes are also important donors to USC's School of Letters, Arts and Sciences and the school bears their name. They have thereby been honored by the opportunity to establish an endowed chair for a crowned Nobel Laureate. They did not have to invest in a faculty member and gamble on the hope that he or she would receive this honor in due course.

Another income stream was derived from retainers and consultant fees from corporations which either already or in the future planned to make use of the methods developed by Arieh and his co-Laureates. This concerns pharmaceutical companies that wish to expand their range of products, and the methods developed by these scientists put the search for promising new medications on a distinctly more rational basis. He also sought professional advice for the investment of his assets, which yields additional income.

Arieh has benefited from a custom developed at other universities by having a special designated parking place that is prominently marked. He has also told me that many of the privileges he had been accorded by the administration had come without his having to request them. He had taken advantage of the advice of other Nobelists and, when necessary, argued for his requests citing precedents at other institutions. He also, wisely, invited the president of USC, C. L. Max Nikias, and his wife, to attend the Nobel Prize Award Ceremony in December 2013 in Stockholm.

Arieh drove a new late-model Lexus that was not bought, but leased by his foundation. In summary, he lives the life of an affluent man, although not really rich when compared to corporate executives or sports and show business celebrities. He also commands a certain level of fame. He remarked that the U.S. media gave limited publicity to the Nobel Laureates. However since he was born in a *Kibbutz* in Israel, he is widely celebrated in that country.

I expect that Arieh will not fall prey to the temptations that have bankrupted many jackpot winners whose lives have undergone a sudden change. His wife, Tamar, is a rational guardian of the purse. Also, I do not expect Arieh to rest on his laurels, but rather he may be expected to stay on course working hard and continuing to make further original scientific contributions. He is now 74 years old and physically vigorous; I expect him to stay in good health for many years to come.

Chapter 20

The Women
in My Life

My mother was, I believe, a beautiful and sensuous but somewhat depressed woman. She probably felt neglected by my father who spent much time on his central interest — dermatology — and more broadly, medicine. Perhaps he also occasionally followed other pursuits.

My mother taught me to put a woman on a pedestal — by bringing me up to serve and support her. I gather that she was not unique in trying to bring up her son to compensate for the inadequacies she perceived in her marital relationship. This orientation, I believe now, colored my relationships with women for much of my life. As a result, I had difficulty being assertive in my relationships with women. On the other hand, I believe that I received a great deal of love and support from my mother in return for the attention she taught me to shower on her.

There was some flavor of a love relationship between us and I believe that I learned sensuality, my capability of deep-seated love for women and my strong sexual motivation from her. This motivation played a central role in my life and enriched it. I am quite certain that I was eroticized in my relationship with my mother and I have had no difficulty having sexual fantasies about my mother in later life. I remember being at a swimming pool when I was ten or eleven and my attempting to stroke my mother's bare thigh. She gently removed my hand and explained that such contact was inappropriate in public. She did not say if it was permissible in private.

ANNE

My first serious relationship that included sexual intimacy was with Anne, a young woman "co-ed" while I was a graduate student at UC Berkeley. We had a lot of fun and passion together and I also experienced much intellectual stimulation with her.

However, we were continually plagued by her psychological problems and her neediness. She had, I understand now, probably suffered from deprivation of parental emotional support during her childhood and early adulthood.

She told me of her pain resulting from a pregnancy and experiencing an abortion.

"It was my child — it was mine!" she said with deep-felt emotion.

I bought things for her, including shoes she needed, since she had difficulty getting the required funding from her parents. My own financial resources were limited. I was a graduate student and lived on a teaching assistant's salary of $120 a month in 1949 with $10 deducted for income tax, and I paid general fees to the university of about another $10 including health insurance. An important bonus of the TA job was being relieved of non-resident's fees, which amounted to $150 per semester. I had some occasional additional income from teaching at Massey's Tutoring School.

Finally, I felt it was all too much and ended the relationship. In retrospect I suspect that I may have sought out aspects of my mother's lack of stability in

women, and this preoccupation led to unhappy end-
ings.

MIRIAM

My first marriage was to a woman whom I found
attractive and who looked up to me as intellectually
superior. This attitude had its roots in our past history in Shanghai where I tutored her when she had to
change schools during wartime. Many parents of my
students had an exaggerated view of me as a superi-
or intellect. I met Miriam again when we both attended a wedding at Hillel House in Berkeley
between an Israeli woman and a young Jewish man
from Shanghai. Miriam had immigrated to San
Francisco with her parents. I was attracted to her
and I was also impressed with her ambition. She had
begun to study at San Francisco State University in
the education department with the aim of obtaining
a teaching credential. We began dating. I visited her
on weekends and stayed in a separate room at their
house. She introduced me to open-air concerts in
Golden Gate Park and we visited museums and saw
movies. We began a romantic relationship which
deepened with time and after several months we
declared our love to each other and began talking of

plans for the future. Miriam's parents were more than supportive, based on their positive view of me as an ambitious and promising scholar. They were at the time struggling to establish themselves financially as new immigrants.

"I see you as a beautiful young woman and am truly attracted to you. I miss you during the week when I am in Berkeley and look forward to being with you on the weekend. Often, I think of a future together. I feel that I am in love with you. Do you ever think of spending the future with me?" I asked Miriam during one of our weekends together, in between exchanges of hugs and kisses.

"I do have similar feelings towards you. As you know, my parents think a great deal of you and would be supportive of our relationship having a future. I have not thought about marriage. I am not sure that I am ready for that level of commitment, but I often feel that I am in love with you," was her response.

"As you already know, I have strong feelings about the Holocaust and the death of millions of Jews killed by the Germans during WWII which I, myself narrowly escaped, thanks to my father's wisdom and drive to flee from Vienna to Shanghai. I have decided to immigrate to the newly established State of Israel and see my future there following my graduation from UC Berkeley. I am at this point practically assured of getting my doctorate following my passing the qualifying examinations and admission to candidacy. I feel confident that I will be able to find a job in Israel based on this qualification. I am fully aware that it would be a big step for you to join me in this adventure."

Miriam responded thoughtfully.

"As you also already know, immigrating to the U.S. has been the fulfillment of a dream which I have nurtured for many years. To give this up and move to a new country and to adapt to a new culture and in addition to learning a new language would be a huge step. I will have to think about this seriously before I can make a decision of this magnitude. The best I can suggest at this point is to leave any further discussion of our future together for another time."

"I agree with you that it will be best to postpone any further consideration of plans for our joint future. Clearly, these are weighty decisions to be made and we must allow ourselves plenty of time for that."

We did, indeed, stay away from further discussion of our future plans for some weeks, but eventually I asked Miriam to make a decision about going with me to Israel and deciding to get married. A week later Miriam told me that she had arrived at a decision.

"I have thought a lot about our plans to get married and going to live in Israel as a couple. I will join you in going to Israel and settling there."

Following this important decision by Miriam, we went about making concrete plans for announcing our engagement. Miriam explained to me that it was important for her parents that I give her an engagement ring to celebrate this step and announce it to their circle of friends. I accomplished this feat by purchasing a satisfactory ring on an installment payment plan extending over a year.

We did not plan any formal wedding ceremony and made an appointment with a judge to have a private wedding in his office in San Francisco with Miriam's parents serving as witnesses. We also did not have the resources to plan for a honeymoon, but my colleagues in the research group, under the leadership of one of them, organized a three-day honeymoon in Carmel, California. Seeing that I did not own a car, one of them drove us there and another picked us up for the return trip.

We rented a small apartment in Berkeley and Miriam transferred to UC Berkeley to continue her studies. She had at first some difficulty adapting to the different academic level but she soon overcame this hurdle. She also found a part-time secretarial job to supplement my income.

As we settled into our life as a couple, Miriam complained that I returned to the laboratory after dinner several times during the week. I had warned her that I would spend one evening a week at the university for a departmental seminar and she had been worried about having to spend that evening by herself. Now she felt abandoned as I returned to the university more often than expected. I explained that working for a doctorate was demanding and required a major commitment. This explanation did not solve the problem and my commitment to my studies and subsequent preoccupation with my career remained a difficulty in our marriage on a continuing basis. Another significant problem was the mismatch in our sex life. It turned out that she did not welcome my sexual advances and even resisted them.

"Miriam, you often invite me to come and stay with you and keep you company while you take a bath. I am sexually aroused by the sight of your body and want to touch you and make love to you but you resist such advances. I find this quite frustrating," I told her.

She did not respond to these protests, and in fact, ignored them. For my part, I began resisting her invitations to keep her company while taking a bath, which eventually erected a barrier between us, and our love life deteriorated.

After my completing my thesis, I officially graduated with a Ph.D. degree in Chemistry. I also applied for and received an appointment as a post-doctoral research associate on a government contract with an appropriate increase in salary. This appointment allowed me to continue my research work and publish the results in peer-reviewed journals.

I also applied for a junior position in the chemistry department at the Israel Institute of Technology, also known as Technion, in Haifa, the northern port city of Israel.

We moved to Haifa in September 1952. In preparation for my teaching in Hebrew, both Miriam and I were sent to a Hebrew boarding school, called *Ulpan* in Naharia, a coastal vacation town north of Haifa. Miriam was enrolled in the beginners' level and I attended the advanced level intensive Hebrew course. We stayed there for four of the five month course after which we moved to our prefabricated house in Haifa and I began teaching. Our first daughter, Debbie, was born in October 1953 and Miriam was occupied for some years with taking care of the baby. She eventually settled into a job teaching English in a private high school, by all accounts led a satisfying life and was well-regarded in the community. We had our second daughter, Judith Tamar, in November 1958, while we were on sabbatical leave in Washington, D.C.

When I considered leaving Israel in 1965, I consulted with Miriam.

"Miriam, I am seriously considering leaving Israel and accepting a position at the University of Southern California in Los Angeles. How do you feel about this?"

She responded: "It is all the same to me. I am satisfied to stay and continue my established life in Israel or I am just as happy to leave and move to the United States to finally fulfill my dream to live there."

We did move to Los Angeles in September 1965. Miriam enrolled in the graduate school at Loyola Marymount University and completed her M.A. degree in education and her requirements for a counseling certificate in 1968. She then took up a teaching along with a counseling job at the Culver City high school and worked there until her retirement.

Our marriage underwent a major crisis in 1970 that I experienced as very unsettling and which eventually, with Miriam's encouragement, led me to a path of seeking counseling and psychotherapy. I pursued this path with great energy motivated by psychological pain. Eventually, instead of leading to a better relationship, this path ultimately led to my decision to seek a divorce. In the course of my self-exploration, I had come to the conclusion that our relationship lacked romance and I wanted out. I moved out in March 1974 and we divorced in 1975 after 24 years of marriage.

I now suspect that I chose Miriam for being undemanding as I saw it at the beginning. I did not want to spend energy on a deep relationship although I did yearn for that at some level. Miriam was a good mother to our two daughters except that she sometimes tried to limit them and keep them close to her. All this is relative to my attitude, and I must say in her defense that she brought them up to be independent by ordinary standards. However, for example, she protested when the older daughter decided at age 20 to go out into the world and return to Israel to do her army service. She did eventually feel neglected by me and, I imagine, suffered from my preoccupation with my work. I suffered from being denied sex, and my feelings of inadequacy as a man, which were implanted in me by my father, were reinforced. I had some adventures outside my marriage in the course of the years but they were such as to be strictly limited in terms of personal involvement. The one comfort was that Miriam was safe — she did not pose a threat, or so I thought.

This world of assumed stability came to a crashing end when Miriam revealed to me that she had had sex with a man. I was crushed, even though this was only a one-time experience without any prospect of recurring. Obviously, Miriam was looking to explore overcoming her aversion to sex and she had given me the signal that she wanted to look for the cure outside our relationship. The incident was followed by a series of adventures on both sides. I felt threatened to the core and came close to the edge of being barely functional, with my level of anxiety ruinously high. From that point on, our relationship was increasingly rocky and unstable. Miriam encouraged me to seek help in psychotherapy, which had begun to interest her, and she thought that this path would lead us to a better relationship. We both eventually chose therapy as a means to find a different level of stability in our lives and came to accept experimentation, including experiences outside our marriage. My pain was a major motivating force for seeking and risking change. I wanted to find more strength in myself to be able to cope with and accept uncertainty and to seek deeper contact with people, both women and men. After a rocky and sometimes exciting period, I came to realize that I wanted out. This came as a surprise to Miriam. Having found a measure of freedom from the sexual inhibitions that had plagued her, she would have wanted to continue some experimentation but wished to hold on to our relationship as primary, or so I understood. I, however, had made the decision to part from our relationship and to adopt the path of seeking self-awareness, in order to find true and deep love and intimacy, of which I felt I had been deprived. This choice brought with it a great deal of emotional pain, as I soon found out,

JINNY

I met Jinny (short for Virginia) at a dinner party hosted by Susan, a former doctoral student of mine at USC. Jinny was a technician at Hughes Laboratory in Malibu where Susan was a research scientist on the staff. I believe it is accurate to say the she shamelessly seduced me, and I loved it. We left the party together and wound up in bed that night. The basis of our relationship was a strong sexual attraction and I was ready and hungry for that. However, I soon came to realize that some puzzling things happened. On a visit to Tijuana, we walked by a cabaret and Jinny expressed interest.

"Let's go in and see what this is about," Jinny said.

And we did. There was a striptease show in progress and we soon left. Jinny then accused me of forcing her to go in and she said angrily:

"Don't do this to me again! I don't want you to push me to do things against my will."

I was taken aback, tried to reason with her and wanted to talk it out, but I failed to establish a reasonable communication with her. She just refused to explain herself and persisted to hold onto her anger. After a while, she calmed down and we managed eventually to return to our normal and even affectionate interaction. But she refused to talk about what I considered our breakdown in communication. As similar incidents occurred later, I decided to end our relationship.

"Jinny, we better stop seeing each other, There is too much turmoil and I am suffering from it," I finally told her.

At that point, Jinny came up with a surprising idea.

"I think that our problems are caused by our not being married. Let's get married and that will fix things."

I did not really believe that this would work, but I was not ready to let go of the deep sexual excitement that I felt when things went well between us, so I was willing to try that. We were married by a judge in Malibu, but our problems persisted. I finally gave up and we divorced and went our different ways. Susan's husband was a lawyer and he managed to negotiate the divorce agreement. Our torrid relationship spanned three years but we only lived together as a married couple for six months.

Eventually I learned to trust my judgment and my feelings. I came to see that Jinny often said one thing and then acted quite differently. She also had a trick of withdrawing suddenly, acting as if she was angry or hurt. I never understood what it was all about and she never would or could tell me. I experienced her withdrawing and I felt as if she had disappeared. This even happened during sex. I was persuaded to marry her because she thought that this would help our relationship, and I was not ready to let go. However, it all went from bad to worse and I made the decision that I had to get out to save my sanity. That ended that relationship. However, I had learned that I could trust my feelings and instincts, and I also was weaned from welcoming seduction as a means of making legitimate and loving contact.

JUDITH

The first time I saw Judith was at the house of mutual friends, Arthur and Gloria, at Arthur's house in Topanga Canyon, northeast of Santa Monica in Southern California. She was sitting on a chair and stood out among all the other friends invited to watch a homemade movie. She was and still is a very beautiful woman, and her erect posture was very special — head high and upraised. I later came to understand that posture was special to her as a practitioner and teacher of the Alexander Technique, a form of physical discipline, which is sought after by actors and musicians to improve their posture. I felt instantly drawn to her, although I did not have the opportunity to speak to her, or perhaps I felt too intimidated to approach her.

The next time I saw Judith was in the Jacuzzi pool at Elysium, a "clothing optional" country club in Topanga Canyon where I was a member. There I saw her in her full glory and was even more impressed and intrigued. This time, I got into the pool and approached her.

"What brings you to Elysium?" I inquired.

"I am giving a workshop here on the Alexander Technique, and this is a recess time," was her response. "I have seen you before at Arthur's house in Topanga and was immediately impressed with your posture and bearing. You truly stood out among the people there. I asked Arthur and Gloria about you, and from them I know something about your background. Your English pronunciation bears the distinct mark of someone who has lived in England."

"Yes, I was born in Czechoslovakia, and my parents were able to flee to England after the German Nazi annexation. We spent the war years there. But now I have to return to my Alexander Technique workshop," and she left.

A short time after this encounter, I called Judith and asked her for a date. She begged off, saying that she was in a relationship that was not entirely satisfactory, but she was not yet ready to give it up. Two weeks later, I received a call.

"Hi, Otto. This is Judith. I want to invite you to join in a double date with my boyfriend and a girlfriend of mine. What do you say?"

I was surprised but was not ready to accept. I thanked her but I wanted to think over her invitation. I called her back and declined, stressing that I wanted to see her but would prefer to see her alone when she would be ready for that. Some time passed without any contact between us, and then I decided to call Judith to try again.

"Hi Judith, I decided to try again to ask you for a date. I just gave up on a relationship and am ready for a new adventure. How is it with you and your relationship situation?"

She told me that she also had given up on her boyfriend and was now free. We agreed that I would pick her up from her home in Santa Monica and that we would go out for dinner.

After filling her in on my life, I explained: "I felt compelled to go to Israel after learning about the Holocaust, but after living there for thirteen years, I returned to California. While living and teaching at the Technion (Israel Institute of Technology) in Haifa, I acquired a Jewish cultural identity and this I find to be a satisfactory resolution. I am now teaching at USC."

After dinner, I took Judith home, and she invited me in. We sat in two stately chairs at some distance from each other. Conversation flowed easily, and we flirted. I was warming up to her, and soon I said: " Judith, I want to sit closer to you."

She wore a soft beige sweater that showed the outlines of her bosom. We moved to a sofa, we touched and I put my arm around her and pulled her closer. She snuggled closer to me, and soon I placed my hand on her breast without sensing any resistance. We kissed, and she suggested that we lie down on the bed and hold each other. I was very excited and pressed her against me.

Judith asked me to turn away from her, and she held me — we felt very close. After a short while Judith murmured:

"For some reason, I feel very excited. Holding you like this from the back is quite erotic."

And so we spent the night together.

We agreed to go out again for dinner the next day. When I arrived to pick her up, I was overcome with excitement when I realized that she wore a semi-transparent blouse, which clearly revealed the outlines of her breasts. I felt embarrassed that the waiter could also see Judith's bosom. After dinner, we hurried back to her house and spent our second night making love. These encounters laid the foundation of an exciting and stimulating relationship that lasted for more than ten years.

Judith's work as an Alexander teacher stimulated her wider interest in exercise and body dynamics and I also benefited from these contacts. One interesting person I met through her was Moshe Feldenkrais, an Israeli physicist who studied in Paris under Frédéric Joliot, who married Irène Curie, the daughter of Marie Curie. They both then changed their last name to Joliot-Curie. Feldenkrais had lots of interesting stories to tell about his interaction with David Ben-Gurion and he became known in Israel as the person who helped Ben-Gurion to alleviate physical pain through his program of exercises. It was said that he got Ben-Gurion to stand on his head. In one of my favorite stories, Feldenkrais responded to Ben Gurion's call to ask him for help and to make an appointment to come to his house. At the time, before they built an official residence for the prime minister, Ben-Gurion lived in an apartment in Tel Aviv. Feldenkrais asked Ben-Gurion for his address, and, in response, he heard Ben-Gurion call out to his wife:

"Paula, where do we live?" Ben-Gurion never went out unaccompanied and was taken everywhere by people who knew the addresses.

Moshe also told me some interesting stories connected to his work for his doctoral thesis in Paris. The scenario aroused some suspicion in me concerning the connection between Israel and France and their cooperation to develop an atomic bomb in Dimona in southern Israel. It is well known that France was the source of the necessary information and support.

Otto Schnepp

When the opportunity arose for me to spend two years in Beijing at the U.S. Embassy, I talked about it with Judith:

"Judith, you have heard me talk about the possibility of my spending two years in Beijing. I have not asked you if you would be willing to accompany me on this adventure, assuming that you would not want to leave your Alexander practice here in Los Angeles. How do you feel about that?"

Judith's response surprised me.

"I've been wondering if you would ask me. In fact, I *would* be willing and even interested in joining you. I could use the time there to study the Chinese physical exercises, including *TAI QI CHUAN* (usually called TAICHI in America) and *QI GONG*; I have been interested in these exercises for a long time. I feel quite secure with my Alexander practice and believe that I would be able to pick it up again without difficulty on my return."

We then turned our attention to the preparations for going off to China and we decided to get married to make things easier for arrangements with the U.S. State Department China Desk, which would be my employer during those two years. We had not planned on marriage before; Judith was not eager, and neither was I, although we had been living together most of the time.

Our relationship was not without problems. We both were strong-willed individuals and had disagreements occasionally. Judith would at times leave in a huff and return to her own house in Santa Monica where she had continued to pursue her Alexander technique practice. After a day or two, she returned to do her laundry at my house. I joked and said that my laundry facilities were an essential asset to our relationship.

During the first year in Beijing, Judith had some difficulty adjusting, and I also was not really helpful because I, myself, had to feel my way and needed to learn in what activities I could include her. Judith participated in a course on Tai Chi and there made the acquaintance of a number of ambassadors and their wives, including the Austrian ambassador, which led to a widening circle of social activities. She also benefited from a Chinese language teacher who translated literature on Chinese physical exercises for her. The second year, Judith connected with the wife of the U.N. representative, who enjoyed ambassadorial stature. She joined her in arranging for Chinese cultural educational activities for the benefit of the diplomatic community.

In the course of these activities, Judith and I started up a friendship with Ruth Weiss, a long-term resident of Beijing from Vienna, who had married a Chinese and was by then divorced. She had lived there throughout the so-called Cultural Revolution (1960-1975) and her experiences during this period were of great interest to all of us. As a non-Chinese, she was reasonably safe from the attacks on educated sections of the population. Ruth also introduced the foreign expatriate community to her favorite Chinese author, Lu Xun, and his writings. He was a popular author, a social critic — something like a Charles Dickens, although he lived in the 20th century, and was particularly well known in the Shanghai area where he lived most of his life. He sported a characteristic mustache.

After our two years were up, we returned to Los Angeles and picked up our former lives. Before leaving for Beijing, we had agreed to make our decision about whether we wanted to continue being married after our return to Los Angeles. We first decided to remain married. However, our relationship became less intense, and we began to move apart. A close friend of mine commented on this:

"You know, Otto, Judith is really a difficult personality. Her narcissistic character trait is an impediment to communication with her. I believe that your relationship is fading. If it were not for your joint experience in Beijing, it would not have lasted this long."

In the course of time, I overcame my fears, learned to assert myself and to insist on space for myself. In my view, Judith began to withdraw, both sexually and emotionally. According to my hypothesis, she did not want that much closeness and intimacy — being married and having a close sexual relationship became too much for her. We went into couples therapy after I had an affair with another woman. I believe that this happened after a period when I tried unsuccessfully to communicate to Judith my frustration and requested that we spend more time together to nurture our intimacy. I felt that she did not hear me and resisted this readjustment. In fact, I believe that we were getting tired of each other and, eventually, I suggested that we divorce and move on. We separated after close to twelve years of relationship and more than nine years of marriage.

EILEEN

Soon after the separation from Judith, I dated Eileen whom I had met through Judith. I knew that Eileen had recently been divorced after a long marriage to a man who had suffered a stroke and undergone a personality change that was the cause of their parting. I had been attracted to Eileen, who was a blond and was beautiful in a different way from Judith, a brunette. As I told her, I liked to look at her, and I found her intellectually stimulating as well as sexually exciting. She also had had a great deal of therapy and was, at the time, studying psychology in evening classes at Loyola-Marymount University in Santa Monica while doing special education teaching. I found her to be a woman who was willing to work on a relationship, something for which I was searching. We were married for twenty years. During this period, we had our problems, but we stuck it out and developed a good and honest relationship.

Things did not move fast at the beginning of our relationship. Eileen was careful and hesitant about allowing sexual intimacy. She even was reluctant to allow me to sit next to her on a couch for several weeks. Eventually, we planned to spend the 4th of July weekend in San Francisco and to stay together at a B&B (bed and breakfast) that she knew in the Haight-Ashbury section. It was a very joyous occasion, and we even smoked some pot that she provided. We initiated our sexual intimacy most successfully with great passion.

We attended a couples therapy group, sometimes over Eileen's resistance, but I learned in the course of time to adjust, to accept Eileen as she was and to enjoy what she was willing to give me. I had a great deal of happiness and love in our relationship and was committed to working on it and achieving continuing improvement. One important contribution, from my point of view, was Eileen's acknowledgement and appreciation of the value of our sex life and her willingness to nurture and support it. I could not have been more grateful for that!

We traveled a great deal, beginning with visits to family of mine in England and Israel and we explored Italy, France and Greece. We travelled by car and visited many parts of Greece where I could read the road signs thanks to my knowledge of the Greek alphabet, which I had acquired in the course of my scientific studies. We made good use of my plan to take an extended trip after my retirement from the USC Chemistry department in 1991. The final stage included a visit to Egypt and a river cruise on the Nile up to the Assuan Dam and beyond to the statues of the Pharaoh Rameses II, which had been moved to higher ground as the water rose to fill the basin behind the Dam.

As we grew older, and our sexual endurance lessened, we were always careful to reserve special time to have physical contact and exchange embraces, and we "made love" in less intensive encounters. We both counted on these times of physical intimacy and closeness. Our sexual ardor dimmed, but we continued to enjoy embraces and hugging.

Eileen had a passion for politics and had her favorite television programs and newscasts. She closely followed elections and had strong views on political candidates. She certainly was a loyal liberal Democrat.

The discovery of the malignant growth in her peritoneal cavity was a terrible shock to both of us, and I suffered great pain from watching her fade away. Her death left a gaping hole in my life.

Made in the USA
San Bernardino, CA
07 May 2017